You Are Cordially Invited
to the Wedding of
Heaven and Earth

You Are Cordially Invited
to the Wedding of
Heaven and Earth

❖

A Simple Guide for Transformation with the Help of the Divine Feminine Spirit

Cristina Braun Jones

Library of Congress Control Number:		2024909460
ISBN:	Hardcover	979-8-3694-2163-5
	Softcover	979-8-3694-2162-8
	eBook	979-8-3694-2161-1

Print information available on the last page.

Rev. date: 06/18/2024

To order additional copies of this book, contact:
Xlibris
844-714-8691
www.Xlibris.com
Orders@Xlibris.com
857230

Photo on book cover by Denver Clark, a brilliant anatomy teacher during my studies at Heartwood Yoga Institute in Bradenton, Florida.

Cover design and technical adviser, Clare Tinsley.

All Bible references are from the King James Bible.

I am not a medical doctor; therefore, please consult your doctor before beginning any form of exercise, alternative healing, or meditation practice.

Book produced by Latina Yoga & Wellness, LLC.

For sessions, please log onto our website, Latinayogawellness.com, or email latinayogawellness@gmail.com, infolatinayogawellness@gmail.com, or tina953@hotmail.com.

"This book is a dawn and an awakening in the soul and conscience of not only women but man who seek to climb one more step in their spiritual evolution."

—Jorge Irula, author of *Silent Longing* (*Amando Desde El Silencio*)

"Cristina is very wise in the ways of her native culture and understands clearly how to navigate the seen and unseen world. She is a brilliant yoga teacher, intuitive, loving, and attentive individual."

—Terri Kowalski, author of *Bees Birthday Surprise*

This work is my prayer for all the women of our beautiful world. I am grateful and joyful in the awareness that we are finally awakening to the sacredness of our mission on earth. We are ready to claim our deserved equality in order to establish harmony and transformation for all.

Divine Mother is ready to assist us with our personal enlightenment, and she is leading the way to transform darkness into light. Please listen to her urgent call: "Now is the time. Awaken, ignite your light, and magnify love."

.

CONTENTS

INTRODUCTION

It is my sincere desire that this account of my life's challenges will help readers overcome their own challenges and access their inner guidance in order to experience life with joy and harmony. It is not my intention to preach or to convert anybody to my truth. I consider myself a truth detective, looking for answers and better ways to navigate this world. I live with the comfort that eventually I can return home to the loving company of heavenly beings.

Since childhood, I have been able to communicate with the heavenly realms by clairsentience (feeling), claircognizance (knowing), lucid dreaming and visions. I believe this was in preparation for this adventure called life. The first years of my life were full of magic in spite of some hardships. This magic was my sustaining grace for the big challenges that life would present to me in later years. These events included childhood sexual abuse, divorce, and a monster called Hurricane Katrina.

Through these friendships with my heavenly companions, I have developed my own strategies to manage and enjoy my life. As a child, I was exposed to several religions and traditions, which opened my mind and helped me to develop my own concept of God. I was close to my paternal grandmother, who was Catholic and devoted to Mother Mary. From her, I learned to appreciate the female side of the history of Christianity.

It was easier for me to relate to Mary than to Jesus since the only influences in my life were female: my mother, grandmothers, aunts, women healers, and my dear godmother. By knowing Mother Mary, I became acquainted with Jesus. I also came to understand that Mother Mary deserves great historical credit. She has my eternal gratitude for listening to my crazy talk and understanding my difficulties in relating to a male God figure.

I hope that by reading about my friendship with this beautiful Lady, you will begin the journey of discovering your own path and asking your own questions. Through her teachings, I have found the great love that Jesus Christ has for humanity, and I have come to understand that his teachings are about enlightenment and enjoyment of our journey here on earth. Unfortunately, we have turned his teachings and death into struggle and division.

My friendship with Jesus and Mother Mary is a true and everlasting friendship. They have manifested themselves to me as friends and guides. They are the most compassionate and loving guides, and they demand nothing in return from me. They have never requested that I worship them or put them up on an untouchable pedestal. With their unconditional love and kindness, I have learned to love them back, and that love is so powerful and sustaining that it is difficult to explain it in written or spoken language.

I know that I have not been an easy case for them. I danced between sadness and anger when my memories got the best of me. I also went through periods of melancholy and a deep longing to be back in the heavenly realms. But my friends have always been ready with their love and understanding, no matter how bitchy or discouraged I have gotten. They have never judged my less-than-evolved decisions. They know I can be a slow learner, and they gently try to open my eyes when I am about to make a wrong decision. Sometimes I listen, and sometimes my stubbornness makes me learn the hard way, but they are always by my side when I call for help.

Because of this friendship, I see life as a school that we attend, with the purpose of multiplying love and advancing spiritually, and some of us take tougher courses than others. I am hoping to graduate with honors and get a scholarship to an easier dimension next time.

My heavenly family has always encouraged me when I get an idea to discover other traditions, and they remind me that we are all brothers and sisters born of the same essence of love.

Due to their understanding, I feel comfortable sharing with other cultures and traditions, and my life is richer from all those experiences. I have enjoyed learning from Mayan shamans in the mountains of Honduras, as well as healers in Costa Rica. Here in the USA, I have studied the gentle teachings of Paramhansa Yogananda, Reiki masters, sound healers, and many other traditions and healing modalities. I treasure my taste for spiritual adventures and feel blessed to have met some wonderful people along the way on multiple planes of existence. I still enjoy going to Mass and to other church services, and I feel comfortable because I now know that I have my own truth within me.

After cultivating their friendship all these years, it is still beyond my comprehension why we humans tend to put God up on some mysterious throne, ready to throw us into a lake of fire for the simple mistake of not finding our GPS in this world.

The heavenly beings I know are illuminated beings projecting only love, understanding, compassion, and care. I have never felt a glimpse of rage, revenge, or a desire to punish me. They have an incredible sense of humor and do their best to put up little signs and roadblocks when something I desire is not for my highest good, but they also light my way when my desire is aligned with my divine plan.

They know that one of my joys is my crazy sense of humor, and they love to share a good laugh and a funny story. I am well known in my inner circle for my love of sleep. I can vegetate in bed for hours at a time, sleeping or reading. But I also enjoy a good party, and I love the company of good friends from many different countries. One day, I was debating whether I should go out with friends for an early dinner and music or meditate and manifest some more writings. Of course, I did not consult with Mother Mary. I just decided that I deserved a night of fun.

I went out, had a good time, and went to bed totally exhausted and planning to sleep until late the next morning. Those were my plans but not hers. I was rudely awakened (she says it was softly) after a few hours of sleep with the command to get up and write.

She would not take no for an answer and motivated me by saying that a special mantra was going to be given to me immediately.

I got up complaining but set out to write, and within minutes, the mantra for the five gifts of the transformation plan was flowing from my tired little hands onto the laptop. I kept writing as I was guided and was able to finish a chapter that I had abandoned a few weeks earlier. Afterward, I was totally energized and filled with incredible joy. After I finished, she directed me to go outside for a special reward for losing my precious sleep.

It was a beautiful winter night, with a full moon displaying the most spectacular light show. There were beautiful rings of light around the moon, and the clouds were forming the most enchanting figures dancing and interacting with the rings of light. The amazing free show absolutely took my breath away, and I felt so thrilled to be alive and in the company of my dear Lady. I was so grateful that I ended up thanking her for waking me up at such a crazy hour. After witnessing her generosity and the power of our magical universe, I went back to bed and had the most restful and peaceful sleep.

After awakening later that day, I was reenergized with the realization that it is time for women to claim our important roles in balancing our world with compassion and harmony, beginning with the history of Christianity, where women were as involved as men were in developing the new path, though they were mostly ignored and discredited in the account of Jesus's life.

It is time to start tearing down those outdated veils and know that we are meant to live in harmony and balance. Collaboration and unity are the prescription for the new era, and women's contributions will be the main ingredient for this new way of life.

When did we become so brainwashed and accept the story that creation is only male energy? If God himself needed Mary to bring Christ into the world, why have women accepted such a small supporting role in Christianity's history for centuries?

I pray daily that humanity will come to realize that the love and guidance of the Mother, or female energy, is necessary for our spiritual and physical well-being—whether we call her Mother Mary, Divine Mother, Quan Yin, Ixchel (Mayan goddess), or any name that resonates with our own idea of the mother. The important thing is to know that it is time to harmonize both sides and create a better experience for all.

With harmony and love, we are building a better world.

My Heavenly Friends

I know that we are all born with the ability to communicate with the heavenly realms, but for some reason, most people forget this innate ability. I consider myself extremely blessed to have been able to keep this communication with my heavenly family, even though I drifted away from them for periods of my life. However, they had been patiently waiting for me every time I came back.

I was the quiet child who would rather read and listen than participate in conversation, and I think this listening was one of the keys to keeping my channels open. I was called shy, stupid, and many others things, but somehow labels did little to bother me. Because of those labels, I was bullied by children and adults, but I laughed on the inside, because the bullies did not have the friends in high places that I had.

Because of my disease-prone body, I preferred to spend time exploring and contemplating nature. I had a rich inner life and was my own best friend. It was easier for me to communicate with animals and Mother Nature than with people. Building my inner life was my way of coping with the latest bout of anemia and many childhood diseases. I was the poster child for every new disease in town.

Later on, I learned that many people who are born energetically sensitive are prone to physical weakness and are able to feel and sometimes carry the toxic emotions and diseases of others. This is also known as being an empath. Occasionally, I slipped into despair, not knowing that I was absorbing the emotions of others or the environment. This has been one of my challenges in this lifetime—to listen and be compassionate to people in need without absorbing and carrying their burdens. I am now learning to protect myself from others' energy while helping them clear their emotions and heal traumas from the past.

My father, who I adored, was an alcoholic and absent most of the time; therefore, his influence in my life was minimal. My mother, being a schoolteacher, demanded perfection, and there was drama and extreme discipline at home. I could talk to my younger sister, who is also intuitive, and sometimes we would spook and impress our friends with our magic; however, for our own protection, we agreed that nobody understood us and that we would keep our knowledge to ourselves. My main refuge was nature and my spiritual friends.

I was raised in a small country village. It was a scenic village in Central America with beautiful rivers and mountains. Ever since I can remember, I would walk down to the river and sit for hours on a beautiful and spiritually nurturing rock. Just by observing the river, I would put myself in a meditative state and communicate with the river creatures and angelic beings.

They had a special sign when they wanted to communicate with me, which was a little noise between my eyebrows, like the buzzing of a bee, accompanied by what felt like a feather tickling my forehead. I would tell my mother the little motor in my forehead was on, and I would just walk into the forest or the few steps to the river. She could not understand this and was afraid for me sometimes, but it was the most natural thing to me, like somebody knocking at my door. Later, when I studied yoga and the energy centers of our bodies, also called chakras, I realized that indeed they were knocking on my intuition door. The communication was two-way because I could call on them as well.

We were outsiders in this little town of rich land but very few conveniences. My mother had been transferred there when I was two years old. She was ordered by the school system to "go civilize those illiterate Indians." She was told that her chances for success were minimal. Several teachers before her had quit, and others had refused the assignment. The school system had no idea that they were dealing with Mrs. Dictator-Warrior-Goddess. She ended up spending the rest of her teaching career there and making true friendships and great progress. By the time she retired, she was a midwife, a healer, and the most beloved teacher of the growing community.

I learned not only from my mother but also from the natives who still knew and practiced Mayan rituals and healings, with touches of Catholic teachings. There were a few landowners from the nearest cities, but the majority could barely read and write. To the casual observer of the city and the school system, they might have seemed illiterate, but to me they were the true essence of knowledge and attunement with Mother

Earth. Their diagnostic tools were their intuition and a stomach massage to detect stagnant energy. Their healing techniques included the use of herbs, massage, and cleansing rituals. They believed that everyone could channel healing through their hands and that a child's hands had the best healing energy. I was blessed early in my life with this knowledge and practice.

My first memory of their medicine is when I was around four. I had hurt my right foot and dislocated my big toe playing soccer. My mother sent me to one of the healers with divine hands, who proceeded to put my toe back into place with just a few hand movements and loving energy. After the session, she instructed me on how to take care of my injury and sent me home with a jar of a homemade mixture that included herbs and oils. She also took my little hands into her hands and declared that I had healing fire in my hands and that I could heal myself. I admired and respected this compassionate healer and totally believed her proclamation that I was a healer. My innocent mind never doubted her words, and I continued my own healing on my injured foot. Her words resonated fully in my heart, and I did not question her command to heal myself. Somehow, I knew deep in my heart that we are all born with this ability. I was so blessed to have such a wise woman remind me of this fact.

Soon after my own healing was complete, I was accompanying my mother on a visit to a neighbor who was in the last stages of a terminal disease, and I was presented with my first opportunity for hands-on healing. There was a gathering of several healers, including one of the village's most admired and trusted medicine women. The healers took me to the dying man's room to help him with the pain. My instructions were that I was to help him die peacefully. The medicine women knew that he was terminal and that there was no point in fighting the inevitable. The mission was to help him die peacefully, aware and in touch with his own reality.

As I laid my little hands on his stomach, his smile told me that he was grateful, and at the end of the session, he signaled that the pain had decreased. In that instant, I was awakened forever to the power of our own energy, and I began to understand the sisterhood of life and death. I learned by watching and doing. There were no written lessons, but the healers were wise and knew that my memory was my best tool, and I was able to retain most of the teachings, a real miracle considering my young age.

After 36 years I went back to my beloved village and to my surprise there was only one surviving medicine woman, the one that had helped me healed my injured toe when I was a child. I was also overjoyed to visit the river and find my favorite rock where I used to meditate and interact with angels and my nature friends.

The moon was their special divination tool, and they could utilize her energy for healing as well as planting and harvesting. They could also predict the weather with incredible accuracy. From them, I learned to appreciate and care for Mother Earth and to be thankful for all the resources that she so willingly provides for us. They were poor in material possessions but rich in joy, gratitude, and magic. The natural resources and the beautiful scenery made up for the lack of money and possessions. Friendships were real, and exchanging supplies and services was the main currency used in those days.

There was another side to their culture, and there were a few who could manipulate energy for sinister purposes. This opened my eyes at an early age to the fact that our choices are powerful and that it is necessary to work with love and to do no harm. I understood that results were sometimes slower with the light, but they were more uplifting and sustaining. I was blessed to also have heavenly guidance, which helped me understand the two sides of the energy.

My heavenly friends taught me how to stay calm and raise myself above the chaos. I learned to detach myself from any situation and just become an observer. Because of them, it was a peaceful existence, and I was left alone to my own discoveries of nature and heavenly realms. My visits with Mother Mary were the highlights of my young years, and I was always happy to tag along with the medicine women and my mother to visit the sick and the terminally ill. I was fascinated by their belief that it was our duty to help the dying cross over in peace and surrounded by loving care. Later in my life, I dedicated many years to the care of the elderly population.

My friendship with Mother Mary was mostly kept secret, because at some point during my childhood, my mother broke ties with the Catholic Church while she was working on coming to terms with her own belief system and spiritual life. However, my mother understood my need for prayer, and she allowed me to go to the rosary meetings, which I adored because I could feel and enjoy the energy of the prayers. The blend of Catholicism and Mayan teachings was fascinating to me because the indigenous people saw God as being everywhere, and there was no conflict at all.

My paternal grandmother, who lived in the nearest city, was the one person I confided in, and she understood my open mind. She used to whisper in my ear, "If there was no Mary, there would be no Jesus," confirming Mother Mary's important role. I spent vacations with my grandmother in the city, and she took every opportunity to teach me her Catholic faith. She was strong in her faith but not blind to the issues that needed to be changed in the church. For attending Mass, I was rewarded with a Sunday treat to the ice-cream parlor, a luxury for many children in those days. She taught me that Mother Mary was just as ascended as Jesus himself. She also made it clear that, even though she had an altar, we were not worshipping statues. The images were just to remind us to strive to be like Mary, who said yes to the petition of her Creator and accepted her mission in life. This was a great blessing to have a grandmother who gave me advice and knew that my inner life was rich and that I needed guidance.

I was also born with the ability of vivid dreaming, and to this day, my guides communicate with me in my dreams. As I grew older, it was easier for them to get my attention in the dream time.

One of my most memorable dreams happened when I was seven years old. My mother used to tell the story that one night, she was checking on me before she went to bed, and I seemed to have been holding a conversation. She said that I was somewhat restless, and I kept whispering in my sleep. She was already worried about my dreams, so I had stopped telling her about my nighttime adventures. She got closer and paid attention, and she said that I clearly stated that since I was seven years old, the number to buy for Sunday's lotto was the number seven. I declared the prediction twice.

The country had a lottery of pick-two-numbers every Sunday. Resourceful individuals would sell raffle tickets that played along with the lotto. My mother bought every raffle ticket in town and a few pieces of lotto (the more you bought, the more you won). The first Sunday, nothing happened, but my mother, being a wise woman, decided that since I had declared it twice, she would buy everything again the second Sunday. On this second attempt, we won every raffle in town, from toys to a cookie jar filled with sweets (my angels know my love of sweets). We also won a small amount of money, which in those days was a fortune. My mother had been worried about finances days earlier, and I must have made a deal with my angels to help us out.

I have never been able to replicate such a wonderful feat, not even after assuring my angels that I would be a good manager of mega millions.

After the sixth grade, I had to move to the city to continue my education, and slowly the city and its allures and dangers replaced my friendship with the heavenly beings, and my spirituality took a back seat to city living. My new life was also a rude awakening after the innocence and peace of my country life.

After I turned eighteen, I moved to the United States, and I let my spiritual life drift and almost disappear. My guides got my attention through dreams, and sometimes I would pay attention.

Life happened. I went to school, learned English, got married, had children, and so on. I was not totally comfortable, and I knew that something was missing, even though I had accomplished many goals and realized several dreams. I felt out of place most of the time, and I knew that it had nothing to do with living in another country; it had to do with my spiritual life. I argued with myself constantly for letting my connection with the divine get weak in the busyness of life. But things were about to get interesting.

A FRIEND KEEPS
HER PROMISE

Something happened in 1988 that would change my life forever and return me to the path of spiritual discovery.

In the fall of 1987, I found out that I was expecting my third child. Those were the days of phone calls and airmail letters. I let several friends know the news. Back in my home country, I had a dear family friend who came to the United States to visit us quite often. I wrote to her and told her that I was worried about the birth since it would be in the summer when my other two children would be home for summer vacation. She wrote back and said, "Don't worry. I was planning a visit anyway, and I will help you until you are back on your feet."

The delivery date came, and what started as a normal delivery turned into an incredible adventure, which seems to be the pattern of my life. I was scheduled for a tubal ligation right after the birth, but for some unexplained reason, two epidurals did not take effect.

As soon as they moved me to the delivery room, a huge hailstorm hit the area. The hospital momentarily lost power, and they went to generator power. There were big balls of hail hitting the hospital windows. The storm damaged cars and roofs and even made an international airliner lose power in midair. It had to make an emergency landing at New Orleans Lakefront.

Right after my son was born, my brilliant medical team decided to give me general anesthesia in order to perform the tubal ligation. They did not stop to think that they were dealing with a small person who had been in delivery for hours and with a blood pressure that has always run on the low side. They performed the tubal ligation, but right after the procedure, my blood pressure collapsed, and they nearly sent me prematurely to the other side. Alarms blared, announcing my imminent departure, and what was supposed to be a short procedure turned into a chaotic battle of life and death. Right after the baby was born, my husband had stepped out for a much-needed cigarette break, but when he returned and approached the nurse's station, he realized by the look on their faces that something had gone terribly wrong. Of course, he was not allowed back in, but he realized that the situation was serious; this was a small hospital, and everybody had gone into emergency mode.

After waking up, I remember hearing that I had given them the scare of their lives. I could read the conflicting signs of fear and relief on their faces. One of the nurses told me, "I have never prayed so much in my life." Thank you, dear lady; your prayers were heard and answered beautifully. The anesthesiologist felt so bad that he never sent us a bill, and my doctor looked totally uncomfortable answering my questions.

I came close to dying, but I do not recall crossing to the light. However, after waking up, I felt total acceptance and love and was not angry at the medical team. My husband, on the other hand, was angry and anxious to learn the truth. After hours of constant care, I was finally brought to my room in the evening. They were continuously checking my blood pressure, but all I wanted was to be left alone and get relief for an acute thirst that just would not go away. I drank water, orange juice, and apple juice and chewed ice, but nothing helped. I felt totally dehydrated and with body pain that seemed from head to toes. The most annoying feeling was a constant sensation of burning in my throat area and chest pains, and I was convinced that a heart attack was flirting with me.

I had been in labor since around five in the morning, and it was getting close to eleven o'clock at night. All the stress of the day was catching up with me. I felt awful, and literally every ounce of energy was leaving my body. I curled up in bed resigned to die because I felt weak, nauseated, and abandoned by my heavenly fiends and disappointed in modern medicine. How I wished that I was with the wise medicine women I knew in childhood.

To my surprise, as I was bargaining with the angels to stop the discomfort or help me die, a new nurse appeared in my room. She was different; she seemed so loving and thrilled to be with me. I remember looking at her and thinking how much she looked like my dear friend who had died a few weeks ago. I did not tell her that, but I knew that she was aware of what I was thinking.

I asked her if she was the midnight nurse, and she just smiled at me. I also asked her if she was going to take my blood pressure, but she had no blood pressure equipment. I told her that I felt like I was dying; I had this terrifying thirst, and nothing they had given me had helped. My throat felt like it was literally on fire.

I kept looking for her name tag, but there was none, and she was not wearing a nurse's uniform either. She was dressed in white, but it seemed translucent—a radiant glow more than a color. She looked beautiful, and her hair was pure sunshine.

In an instant, and without any movement, I had a colorful drink in my hand. It was the most delicious and refreshing juice I have ever tasted in my entire life. There is no way to describe the satisfying and healing power of that drink. It tasted like a combination of every fruit that I love. The debilitating thirst instantly went away after the first sip. I sat up with newfound energy and realized that this was no ordinary drink, and this person was no ordinary nurse.

I finally had the nerve to tell her, "You look just like a friend of mine who died last month." This is the friend who had promised to come up and visit to help me with the baby. She gave me a beautiful smile, and instantly I realized that I was experiencing a visit from the other side. My friend was a beautiful woman, but a vicious cancer took her life in her late forties. This woman in front of me was in the prime of her youth and beauty, and I saw no signs of the destruction caused by the cancer she had fought for several years.

As soon as she knew that I knew, she looked straight into my eyes, and in that instant, I had no doubt that I was experiencing life from another plane of existence. The compassion emanating from her eyes was beyond description. This compassion filled my entire being, and for a moment, there was no pain, no worry—just pure bliss. I finally understood the bliss of oneness that had been discussed with my friends of like mind. I was one with wisdom, love, and peace and everything good in the universe. I felt like I was melting into unconditional love and total peace. Even the hard hospital bed felt like the softest and most magical cotton. The hospital room was glowing with soothing light. The discomfort of my body was nonexistent. My body felt totally relaxed, my mind was in the most peaceful and silent place, and my soul was in a state of immense and indescribable joy. In that precious instant, I knew that life is eternal, and joy and love are ours forever. Everything made perfect sense. I also realized that there is no death, because she was the same generous and loving person I had known, but now she was without the baggage of pain and fear.

I asked her about her family, and she let me know that she was doing different work now and that everything was as it should be. I also asked her if she missed her family, and she told me that everybody was fine and doing what needed to be done. She said that the work she was doing now was necessary for the greater good of humanity.

When I asked her if she was coming back to see me again, she just gave me a beautiful smile and told me that she is always with me. In fact, she had even been by my bedside when things went wild in the delivery room.

I got the feeling that the unseen world is very near us and that our loved ones never leave us. My mind had a million questions for her, but I felt that all the answers were contained in the unconditional love that I was being gifted with in that precious moment. I now knew that everything always works for our benefit, and every experience is necessary for the lessons that we agreed to learn. I was just happy enjoying every second of this all-knowing and all-loving experience.

After a few minutes of showering me with all that love and compassion, she sat by the windowsill. I invited her to come back the following night, and she gave me her unforgettable smile and disappeared as fast as she had appeared in my room. I wanted more of her sweet company and to be able to see her by my side forever, but I knew that it had been a once-in-a-lifetime gift. I immediately experienced a state of complete gratitude for such a privilege. (I have felt her presence and have had her give me encouragement in my dreams but never again in the visible realm.)

After she disappeared, I realized that we did not use spoken language. I cannot say that our communication was by thought either, because it was just a knowing. There was absolutely no effort in our communication. The best way to describe it is that we were both on the same page, and we were accessing a fountain of divine, universal wisdom that knew everything. There was no need to think anything. We both had the same information. What a beautiful state of being—no effort to think or do anything, just pure knowing and joy. To this day, I crave that feeling of not having the burden of thinking and figuring things out.

My entire being felt illuminated and happy, and my first thought after she disappeared was that I did not have my journal to write this extraordinary experience. I decided that I would stay awake, for fear of forgetting it; however, I fell asleep immediately and had a peaceful and renewing rest.

In the morning, I was thrilled that the details of my encounter with the other side were as vivid as the night before. I asked the nurses and aids if they had seen this beautiful lady who came to visit me, but they all gave me questioning looks. My hospital stay had already caused enough drama, and for fear of being labeled crazy, I dropped the subject. I already had a few labels from childhood and did not want to own any more.

I looked in my room for the beautiful drink container, but I saw only hospital cups and a pitcher of ice water. The mattress was back to being uncomfortable and hard, and the room was boring and cold. *What a letdown*, I thought. I had to find every drop of strength in my body to survive the day. I wanted to be where she was. I wanted that carefree feeling again and to be in that place of total peace and security. I knew I had to go on in this imperfect world for the well-being of my children, and I took comfort in the fact that when my time of transition came, I would be going back to a loving and compassionate home.

Except for a few people of like mind (which included my younger sister), I kept my secret but lived with the realization that my dear friend kept her promise. When I had written to her about my pregnancy, she was already in advanced stages of cancer, and we both knew that her trip would not be possible. Her words in her letter were a promise that I did not understand at the time—she would come and see me anyway. I wrote back saying, "I am looking forward to your visit." She died about six weeks before my son was born, but like a true friend, she kept her promise, and I know that, somehow, she influenced my outcome after my brush with the other side. She knew my children needed me, and she nursed me back to health that awful night when human drinks could not help me.

The image of her radiant beauty and peaceful smile is imprinted in my memory forever. I pray always for another glimpse of that complete feeling of love and compassion. I know that I had the privilege of an open portal to heaven that night, and better yet, I know that my dear friend is at peace and more beautiful than ever, continuing a life of service in a different way.

No matter how sad I get or how difficult life becomes, all I have to do is go back to the memories of that night and regain a sense of optimism and trust that the divine plan for our lives must be preordained. Thank you, my dear friend, for keeping your promise. What an honor to have you as my friend.

After that experience, I started seeking answers again. I began reading spiritual books and searching for answers. My husband thought I had gone over the edge with my fascination with life after death, but I never confided in him the reason for my search. He was furious at the doctors, and I did not want him knowing that I had been closer to death than he had imagined. Besides, my alternative way of healing and life did not exactly match with his.

Life went on, and I got busy raising children, but I experienced periods of sadness. I was sad for the confusion about death and my fear of telling my story. I had a glimpse of life after death through my loyal friend. During one of the sad periods in my life, I decided to teach myself to meditate again, and that has been a saving grace, helping to keep me grounded in the good times and the not-so-good periods of life. During meditation, I have been blessed to be able to experience unity and instants of that peaceful feeling again. That beautiful visit was a gift that I treasure more and more as I get older and have more time to reflect on the unity and wonder of the universe.

Life went on, and I went in and out of communication with Jesus and Mother Mary. I became angry with them after I got divorced, and I blamed them for not saving my marriage, for losing my employment, for Hurricane Katrina, and for every bad event of my life. But by then, I knew that even when I was angry, keeping my channels open was an essential ingredient to coping with life's twists and turns.

They were not about to give up on me, and little signs started to appear in my life, telling me they were keeping their eyes on me.

MY ROAD TO
TRANSFORMATION BEGINS

The signs started to appear one by one. I was praying one day, and I decided I should get back into my habit of saying the rosary. I had lost all my rosaries during one of the floods I lived through. After I finished rebuilding my home, I made a mental note to get a rosary, and I also starting looking for the best corner in my home for my new altar. A few days later, one of my nieces came to visit me, and to my surprise, she presented me with a beautiful rosary. She told me that someone had given her this gift, and she thought that I would be the right person to own this rosary.

While thanking her, my mind was already questioning if this was a sign from my dear Lady. Since my niece rarely visited me, and she came over just to give me that beautiful gift, I decided that this was definitely a spiritual sign. Strike one for Doubting Mind. Team Spirit was overjoyed.

Sometime later, I went to visit my older sister, and she was very excited about a present that she had for me. She had a beautiful, vintage statue of the Blessed Mother that she was lovingly saving for me.

A few weeks later, I met another one of my nieces for lunch, and she was wearing a beautiful necklace with pictures of Jesus and Mary. I complimented her on the beautiful necklace, and she immediately took it off and handed it to me, telling me, "It is yours because I love you." Strike three for Doubting Mind. Game over. Team Spirit celebrated, and I was really paying attention then.

Knowing there was more chaos coming into my life, Mother Mary pointed my way to a Carmelite spiritual center located in a small city next to mine. I became a regular visitor, taking classes and doing retreats and strengthening my spiritual life. I spent many beautiful days before and after Hurricane Katrina learning from these beautiful nuns and their guests.

I will never forget Sister Christine, who helped me understand the real meaning of forgiveness and compassion for myself and other human beings. What an oasis of peace and love to overcome any great storm that life throws at us. The center is a place full of prayer and love and communion with Spirit—not to mention the beautiful landscape and special corners for solitude and meditation.

After more or less putting my life back in order after Katrina, I organized my new apartment and decided to take a trip to California, to a beautiful mountain retreat where they follow the teachings of Paramhansa Yogananda and where I had recharged my batteries once before. Nature and meditation have always helped me get back on track when restarting my life, which has happened quiet often.

I called to make reservations, and the clerk asked me if I preferred any particular room (they have rooms dedicated to different religions), and I said, "Not really. Just make sure it has a private bath." (No more sharing a bathroom with twenty or more people like I did in the aftermath of Katrina.)

The day before my trip, I was watching a show on TV, and they were showing a little booklet of a certain miracle novena. They were narrating personal stories of great miracles and explaining how Mother Mary listens to all of our prayers and pleas for mercy. I made a mental note to look for the booklet after returning from my trip. When I arrived at the retreat, I was surprised to find that my room was decorated with images of Mother Mary. She wanted to make sure that I stayed on track this time, and her soft whispering is now constant.

I had a great time on the trip, made some lifelong friends, and made better contact with my heavenly friends. I was completely reenergized and ready to get on with my life again.

When I got back home, my boyfriend had a present for me—the little booklet with the novena. Before I left for my trip, I had never mentioned to him that I was planning on searching for this precious item. Somebody had given him the little booklet at work. Talk about persistence from my dear Lady. I was now convinced that Mother Mary was eager to guide me, and I definitely wanted to be her devoted friend for the rest of my days on this earth and beyond.

When you are ready to begin your path of discovery, please pay attention to the little miracles and synchronicities that appear in your life. Your guides and angels will make themselves known once you declare your intentions. Make sure to state your petition clearly, that you are lovingly waiting for their guidance. Always keep in mind that they respect free will but are totally thrilled when you ask, and they will go into action when their assistance is requested. It saddens me that religions have done a great job in keeping us away from the great system of heavenly helpers who are always waiting and ready to help.

FROM A FEMALE
POINT OF VIEW

Note to readers: Mother Mary appears to me often and speaks to me as a friend. Her favorite time for contact is very early in the morning. She awakens me by the invigorating scent of roses and the magical feeling of a loving embrace. The feeling of her unconditional love is always with me. These are some of our conversations.

After our friendship of so many years, I am eternally grateful for your assistance in telling my story, and in doing so, maybe we can help others clear past traumas and enjoy a more fulfilling life. I am totally thrilled that my internal joy is still present after such an up-and-down life, and I hope that my trials and tribulations can help others get closer to their inner joy and peace. I will do my best to translate your guidance into understandable, easy language, and I hope to download and convey your advice clearly. Any real or perceived mistakes are my own; however, all my love and enthusiasm are poured into this project. For clarity purposes, all your answers will be in quotation marks.

"You will do just fine, my dear. You have the right ingredients: love and enthusiasm. There are no mistakes, only teachings that need to be explored, and then pass them along to others to do their own exploring. I am also thrilled that you are learning your lessons and are willing to share your life's experiences to assist others in finding their own joy and understanding."

I like that, dear Mother—only teachings, no such thing as mistakes. I would like to start with an account of your life on earth and your side of the story from a female point of view. I have had visions of having had a life in that era, but my memories are not complete yet. Can you tell me what really happened after the crucifixion? Did people get along, or was it the usual struggle of people attempting to get control and power?

"There were disagreements before and after the crucifixion concerning who would lead the new movement, and he knew it and admonished them often."

Did Jesus have female disciples?

"There were many female disciples. He taught personal salvation. Everyone was responsible for his or her learning. He trusted men and women equally and had great respect for the female role within the family and community. This trust in women was a major reason for discord among his disciples, followers, and political leaders."

How did he want the church to look after his death, and did he choose only a few to lead the new church?

"It was a teaching movement, not a church. We were to share duties and care for each other. The teachings were about divine love and unity, about the kingdom of heaven within, and about eternal life. This knowledge would bring peace and security."

I believe some truths were hidden from the real story, but I love some of the accounts of the life of Jesus. At the crucifixion, he tells you, "Behold your son," and he tells one of the disciples, "Behold your mother." This indicates to me that he wanted cooperation and unity, but unfortunately, humans turned his sublime mission into competition and disharmony.

"He emphasized unity, love, and compassion, and he taught that male and female were totally equal and complementary of each other. He also taught that every person is complete and capable of achieving greatness by the grace of God. If you understand that you are born complete and capable of sheer joy, you live life with genuine happiness, and your human relations will be total enjoyment without trying to achieve happiness from others or for others."

My paternal grandmother taught me your love, compassion, and intercessory power. However, most churches and pastors totally ignore this point and disregard your gift to humanity, which absolutely drives me to my highest anger level.

"Your dear grandmother was right. I was gifted with the grace to ask on behalf of others, and I know that you understand this point because you love the story of the first miracle, where I was asked to approach him concerning the wine."

Yes, and you know that I love wine. I totally understand because if our bodies are operating in lower vibrations, we cannot reach the higher dimensions necessary to access divine light or the Christ energy. The organizers of the wedding in Cana did not have access to him, but you, being his mother, had sure access to him. You were given the gift to descend to our level and lift our prayers to the highest point. I really get angry at how people misinterpret your willingness to help humanity, with the gift that you rightfully earned. Another disservice to women by the patriarchy, which has worked beautifully for them but has kept women enslaved as second-class citizens for centuries.

How did they manage to ignore and discredit women? Mary Magdalene was made out to be a prostitute. I do not remember reading of many male followers around at the crucifixion, but the women stayed to witness it all. I also see there were many women with financial means supporting his ministry, and several of these women are mentioned in the Bible. This tells me that women were as involved as men in his ministry.

"The historians later on managed to diminish the female contribution. After the crucifixion, the women worked tirelessly on keeping up the faith and his teachings intact. We had more sympathy and respect from religious and government rulers. We did our best to keep the men safe and alert. They were totally devastated by the crucifixion, and it fell on us to comfort them, keep them informed, and plan the future of the new path.

"Let me emphasize, dear one, that the time has come for the divine feminine to reemerge and bring harmony to the new world, and it is up to women like you to bring this truth to light."

Oh, my dear Lady, that sounds to me like an incredible mountain to climb. How do we bring this truth to light without offending the present order?

"By doing what you are doing, my child. Anchor your light in inner strength and wisdom and ask for guidance from the Divine Feminine Spirit and know that we are eager to assist humanity. My beloved Mary Magdalene has always been ready to teach and to guide women to their inner strength and wisdom. Her real story is a mystery worth uncovering. When women awaken to the truth of their mission, they will awaken to their own majestic power. My beloved ladies, it is time to start getting together with other women and mapping out the new world. Be diligent in operating from your divine feminine nature, and changes will automatically come your way."

Would you say that we are better off when we access our feminine wisdom and function truly in our own power, instead of trying to conquer the world by imitating the actions of men?

"You are getting there, my child. Women are powerful beyond belief. When you know the magnificent and important role that you were designed to play for the highest good of our majestic universe, you will be unstoppable. Please do not see men as the enemy or dark creatures. They will become your allies once they understand also the urgency of a new way of life. It is a united effort, not a new war."

That makes total sense to me. Humanity has started enough wars already. I believe that women deserve great respect and admiration. The miracle of birth was entrusted to us because of our inner strength and capacity for love. The sooner we claim this respect, the better off we will be.

"You are so right, my dear. It is imperative and most urgent for the healing of the planet to recognize women's blessed role in the creation of the miracle of life."

Who were the strong candidates to lead the new movement? Did he assign roles, or was there total chaos trying to grab power after the crucifixion?

"He had trained everyone to share and collaborate in the mission. It was meant to be a way of life that would lead to total transformation of the human being. Every follower was capable of teaching to others because the main teaching was to discover the divinity within. He had blessed a small group, which included Mary Magdalene and others, with special knowledge and techniques to carry on."

What was your assignment?

"My assignment was to be a guide and adviser to all and to make sure that his teachings were passed on to others with truth and love."

What was the main message?

"The main message was to spread the good news of the kingdom of heaven on earth. He wanted humanity to know that your search is for unity with your divinity and that you arrive on earth to participate in creation and remember that unity. When you create with love and share with gratitude and compassion, you are contributing to creating heaven on earth."

It sounds simple enough. Why did it get so complicated?

"The power struggle came when some followers wanted the message to be on salvation after death, and most of the women wanted to concentrate on transformation for a better earth life. The women understood the everyday struggles and wanted the message to concentrate on awareness to attain well-being and joy during earth life, which was a truth that he emphasized daily. Also keep in mind that not all of his followers, male or female, understood the real message of salvation clearly."

Was salvation after death emphasized to keep us in fear?

"He taught personal advancement for your earth life and the afterlife. He wanted humanity to know that suffering was a human creation, and he knew the technology to save you from suffering. Salvation for your earth life is to learn to create from love and to enjoy the material plane. Salvation in the afterlife is advancing your spirit to higher states of wisdom, bliss, and choice. Salvation after death has been totally misinterpreted and used to plant fear and suffering in people's mind. By living a life of peace and love, you are advancing your progress on both realities. The good you do on earth is magnified in every level of existence."

Oh my God, I am afraid to ask what happens to the bad that we do on earth. Is it also magnified?

"It is certainly so, my dear. The only difference is that it is only magnified on the earth plane because that type of energy will not penetrate the upper realms of existence. Most humans live in fear, and that creates insecurity and hate. Hate creates jealousy and violence and so on."

I see. In other words, since the result of our mischief stays on our side of town, we are pretty much suffocating in a sea of accumulated wrongdoings. Now I know why you are always insisting that we bring light to darkness in order to start creating the right way, or we will keep creating hell on earth instead of heaven on earth.

"You have understood the teaching, my dear. The urgency of spreading the good news of the light is to stop the multiplication of the darkness brought on by fear and ignorance and to shift to the light, and the sooner the better."

How do we stop creating hell and move on to the business of Christ's mission of creating heaven on earth?

"When you create from fear and greed, you have not realized that you are a part of a divine master plan that has based creation on love. Living in fear creates unfavorable conditions because you have not discovered the greatness hidden within your own being. Creating hell is being unable to confront your fears and masking reality with addictions, false power, and uncontrolled acquiring. If you understood that without you, the giant divine puzzle is hurting, then you would get on with your divine mission quickly."

I see, dear Mother. We need to realize sooner than later that we are divine essence and that even though each individual is unique and different, we are united by the same essence.

Is Christ upset with humanity because we have not done a good job with his teachings?

"He has the most compassion and love for humanity and works constantly at sending love to the world, and he delights in people's efforts of transformation by whatever path they chose."

Being a Christian to me should be a joyful experience. But I know many Christians living in extremely difficult circumstances. Why is it so difficult being a Christian?

"It only seems difficult because of the rules and regulations added to the path by power-hungry leaders. His way is simple. Seek the kingdom by looking within. Improve your circumstances by educating yourself in the ways of the world, but you also need to learn and apply your divine gifts and rights. When he said, "Give to Caesar what belongs to Caesar and to God what belongs to God," he was advising humanity to respect the rules of the world and to use common sense. However, he was also saying to liberate yourself from the world's suffocating rules by the wisdom from divine light."

That seems like great advice to me. I have always thought that following God's way should be simple and enjoyable because we already have enough rules from the world, beginning with the rules we receive from our parents—sometimes wise and sometimes totally misguided.

I know that he is complete love and understands our challenges, but does he hurt when people do not believe in him?

"His wish for humanity is that his teachings would be understood. By learning the system that he taught, the world would have peace, love, and respect for all. He works constantly on behalf of love and knows that humanity is at the beginning of a new awakening, where all his teachings will finally be understood and implemented. The power of love is slowly fueling this awakening and transforming outdated beliefs for the healing of individuals and the planet. Please do not be discouraged by the chaos and destruction that you see. In some inner level, the ones who want change by force know that a new world is coming. They just do not understand that help is available to produce change in an orderly and compassionate way."

Is he disappointed when people choose another path?

"He rejoices in every one who reaches enlightenment. He is pure love, and he believes that every human being is deserving of his love and compassion. When you are pure love, you have no room for judgment."

I get it. So we are the ones who think, *My way or no way*. We must look so selfish and ignorant to all the advanced masters.

"We prefer not to judge but to work always for unity and peace for all. Any form of prayer is always cherished. We know no envy or competition, and we are grateful when our help is requested. We are always ready to assist and comfort humanity."

Are all the advanced masters friendly with each other, and so they party together in the higher dimensions?

"We all work on the mission to give love and understanding to everyone and to help establish the power of love and cooperation for the benefit of humanity. We rejoice in humanity's successes and advances, and we notice when backward steps are taken. We diligently send light to the world to illuminate the way."

What is the biggest misconception about your life and Jesus's life?

"That he taught a gospel of poverty and suffering. He knew his lineage on both realities and was given many treasures at birth, enough to educate him and let him travel on his spiritual journeys."

So he was born with a 529 plan and was well educated?

"Yes, you can say that. He not only had wisdom from within, but he received the best education a child could have. He had many benefactors who had his well-being in mind."

Why do they imply that he was poor and that it is better to be poor than wealthy?

"He loved to teach the poor how to access a better life; therefore, many of his followers were the oppressed, the sick and the poor. But he also had wealthy followers looking for a more fulfilling spiritual life. His teachings on the marriage of spirit and material realms were welcomed by all the classes of society."

He had friends in high and low places and in between?

"People were totally fascinated by his wisdom and compassion for the human condition. He knew that love was the answer, whether you were rich or poor."

I still think that it was more convenient to make him a poor man so the masses could identify with him more. Am I right?

"That was part of the changes made by the ones who took control of the history later on. But he never preached a gospel of poverty. He wanted people to learn to live life to the fullest and to understand the marriage of heaven and earth. When you understand the sacred union, you enjoy creating, guided by Spirit and sharing from your heart. When you create guided by Spirit, you have no room for senseless acquiring or unhealthy habits. You enjoy the process of bringing your creation to the world. You also enjoy teaching others and sharing from your abundance of heavenly and earthly blessings."

I get a picture of him moving easily among rich and poor and being invited to rich and poor gatherings. I imagine that the wedding at Cana was the wedding of important and wealthy people, and his miracle of turning the water into wine was to avoid a major disaster. The wedding planner must have been in big trouble, having run out of wine.

Many people think that this was his wedding to Mary Magdalene. I have never asked you this question because I have never felt the need to know. This information would not alter my admiration and love for him and his mission. However, I have never thought that this was their wedding because such an oversight would never happen at Mary Magdalene's wedding. I know she is the queen of beautiful details.

"That miracle has multiple teachings, and you are slowly getting to the true meaning of those teachings."

What was the biggest mistake made by the followers after he left?

"Moving away from love and turning to fear. Humanity would be totally different if they had followed the plan as originally conceived. However, we knew that it would take time for the complete truth of his teachings to come to life."

We humans always screw things up royally. What is the plan exactly?

"The plan has been all along to teach humans their divinity and the knowledge of letting Spirit guide you for a more enjoyable journey on earth. And the key to the plan is looking within and accessing the light that ignites every detail of creation. The kingdom of God is within, but it is also everywhere; however, you start by looking within and igniting your own light. By working on your personal enlightenment, eventually you can show others the way of the light.

"Humans have a divine and sacred mission, and when they forget it, life becomes complicated. This forgetting makes you prone to developing feelings of lack, fear, and despair. When you know your divine mission, you are aligned with creation, and life flows easily and joyfully."

What is the meaning of the teachings that we cannot get to the father except through him? I have trouble understanding this passage. What would happen to the millions who have died and will die without ever hearing of him or his teachings?

"This has been misinterpreted for centuries. His teachings are not about fear and death. They are about the Christ substance within him, which is the same substance that is in every human being. He wants humanity to know that every human being is just as valuable as the ascended masters in the overall scenario of creation. He wants humanity to know that you are capable of great works and performing miracles, just like he does. Creation is totally grateful to you for undertaking your earth mission, and the support system has always been in place to help you fulfill your sacred agreement.

"He wants to awaken humanity to the importance of your lives on earth and to give you the knowledge for accessing a better way to perform your sacred mission. He wants you to know that a better way to live is to know how to create and to enjoy your mission on earth. The minute you realize that access to the substance of creation is your divine right, you have reached the Father or the infinite light of creation."

Beautiful. I think I get it now. I access my light and divine rights through his teachings; therefore, he is my provider for accessing my own light. In other words, his mission was and still is to teach us how to access the Father or the originator of the light. By learning his system, he becomes our link to salvation from our struggles in this reality, because salvation on the other side is our right, since spirit never dies. If more of us get this truth, then there will be more harmony and love in this world. Am I getting this?

"You are definitely learning, my dear. He taught that every one of you is capable of performing miracles if you realize that you arrive on earth with your pilot light in perfect working order. Your assignment is to discover the switch that ignites that light. And that should be an adventure, not a painful experience."

This is why I get really upset with churches, my Lady, because they teach that we are sinners and not worthy of God's grace, instead of teaching people how to find their guiding system once and for all. I now know that his teachings are the power source for my navigating system, and this assistance comes with no monthly fee and a no-hassles return policy.

However, once I use his system, I fall in love with it, and I become a lifetime, faithful customer. It is so simple and so beautiful. Is like when I go shopping; if I like the store, I become a repeat customer.

"And we both know that you are an expert and dedicated shopper in many worlds, and I love your clear and sincere review. In due time, my dear, the norm will be self-transformation. Remember—for everything, there is a reason and a season. In the meantime, change your own universe and show others the way to the light."

Thank you for the shopper compliment. You know I will go to extremes to find a good bargain, materially and spiritually. Please excuse my sarcasm with organized religion and fearmonger preachers.

"I understand, my dear. But you would have to admit that when you did not get any answers in the churches, you developed an urgency to search on your own. The churches were your starting point, and if you look at it that way, they did you a great deal of good."

Well, if you put it that way, I guess I should be thankful for that. My search adventure has been interesting, to say the least, and I have met wonderful human beings along the way. I love the subtle ways that you teach me the lesson without offending the churches. Let's continue with enlightenment please. What is really the meaning of the kingdom of heaven within us?

"It is remembering who you are and living a life of harmony and nonattachment. It is finding that place within you that is silent but full of wisdom and love."

And disharmony comes when we cannot decipher our master plan because of the confusion of the world and the nonstop chatter of our minds?

"That is correct. Your assignment is to remember that you come from the divine and to integrate every aspect of your being in order to navigate your life with joy and success. When you remember who you are, you have reached the Father, or divine intelligence, and you are capable of following your divine plan and fulfilling your mission."

OUR EARTH MISSION

What is our earth mission, and why do we decide to come to this difficult plane of existence?

"This is not easy to grasp when you are confused by the distractions of the material plane. But you do it out of love and respect for creation. Our Creator loves to create, and you are invited to share in the joy of creating heaven on earth. The challenges outlined in your sacred contract are part of the plan for your inner growth and spiritual expansion.

"You are so loved by divine creation, and you are so grateful for that love that you do not mind a small stop on earth in order to contribute to the expansion of the magical universe. It is a complicated but exciting adventure, and souls are always ready for a challenge. The lessons are carefully mapped out before you arrive on earth. It is also agreed that by experiencing the physical body, the information of your divinity will be temporarily hidden from plain view."

We trade wisdom for the pleasures of the physical body, and we take advantage of a free round trip. Then we embark on the adventure of remembering who we are and where we came from?

"Yes, my dear, you are excited for the opportunity to create and use your talents on the material plane. In the spirit world, you create by divine intelligence, and you help guide those on the material plane. Creation on earth is totally different because you have to learn different strategies, such as focusing and planning. You are totally aware of that when mapping out the plan for your mission, and you know that the challenges and lessons are necessary for the highest good of all."

In other words, we leave Eden to experience the material plane and its pleasures, knowing that our wisdom will be as elusive and clever as the snake. And we agree to this game of hide wisdom and find it again?

"Yes, my dear, because getting back to Eden while still on your earth journey is the ultimate spiritual accomplishment. And coming back to the spiritual realm with that accomplishment admits you to unimaginable levels of love, choice, and wisdom."

I see. This trip down here is inescapable because we don't want to offend creation, and we want to play the game and return victorious?

"Yes, you are eager to fulfill your mission and excited to advance creation and magnify love. And once you find your guiding system or you make your exit from earth, you realize that it is a thing of beauty and extremely brief."

We might as well get on the merry-go-round and enjoy the ride. I guess even after all our troubles, it has its allurement and joyful moments. Can we change the plan that we bring to earth if we find that the challenges are too difficult?

"It is totally up to you, my dear. You are equipped with the tools to do so, and heaven will assist you with that if you so wish. We pray for you and encourage you that your changes will enhance life on earth and not detract from it."

How do we go about changing our contracts without dishonoring our sacred mission?

"Great questions, my dear. Your light is shining bright this morning. The first thing you need to do is ask for divine guidance. Observe the patterns that keep repeating in your life. Make the decision that you wish to discontinue the lesson. Create a meditation, a ritual, or a ceremony for this specific purpose and know that your wishes are totally honored by the universal laws. Your success is our ultimate joy, and your guides are always at your service. Make the commitment that you wish to transform suffering into joy and know that a better outcome is your divine right and it is always possible."

Thank you, dear Mother. In other words, we are allowed to drop the class if it proves to be too big of a burden. And the steps to dropping the class are decision, action, and knowing that a change will take place.

"That is correct, my child. Remember you are on earth to enjoy the experience and to contribute to creation for the good of all. Suffering will not be an option if you accept this truth. Remind yourself that when you mapped your trip, it was a joyful event and that it is your divine right to preserve that joy."

If we mapped out our journey very carefully, why are some people better creators than others?

"The better creators have aligned themselves correctly with spirit, and they focus on what they wish to create. They remember the mission better and are able to access the reservoir of divine intelligence where all the answers exist. They have overcome major lessons in previous lifetimes or in their present one. Always remember there are different levels of progress for everyone; therefore, comparing your successes or failures to others is not the best use for your energy."

It seems that successful people have a clear window to the spirit world, and on some level of their mind, their instruction manual is readily available.

"Yes, my dear. They remember their divinity and have learned to tap into the energy of the spiritual reality. And once you have mastered the use of this clear window and apply the knowledge to your everyday life, it is easier to build success after success."

It sounds like the energy of success expands and attracts more success. And we are now talking about the law of attraction. Is this law a lot of talk, or does it really work? And where do I buy the glass cleaner to make my window crystal clear?

"Well, my dear, I would describe this law as the law of remembering and cocreating. Remembering that you are a citizen of heaven gifted with the power to cocreate on earth. When you know this truth, you are delighted for the opportunity to create abundance for yourself and humanity. When you know that you are divine, you are pure joy, and when you are joy, you automatically turn on your guiding system to receive everything you need to create and expand your joy. Heaven rejoices when you use your creative talents for your own benefit, sharing with others and improving the world."

It seems to me that when we remember who we are, we can sort of copy and paste. Has everything already been created, and all we need to do is download it? But what about attracting misery and tragedy? Is that already created too?

"It is not as simple as that, my dear, but I like the copy and paste analogy. Anything that you can imagine can be created. And if you believe that you can copy and paste, then so it is. However, remember some lessons have to be learned for the overall success of your divine mission.

"The greatest spiritual progress comes from the most difficult lessons. Please do not judge yourself or others for the appearance of misuse of the universal laws, because in the overall plan of our beautiful universe, every lesson learned is magnifying love and wisdom. When you decide to focus on enlightenment, you will get a better picture of the plan. You will understand that it was necessary to know the depth of despair to advance your mission and be a good guide for others who need encouragement to find their inner light. Usually, the wisest teachers are teaching from their own experiences. Also remember that when you are operating with the wrong tools, unnecessary suffering is created."

It sounds to me that we should be grateful for all the lessons, good or bad, because there is growth hidden in all of them. I guess you make sense, because I have been to hell and back. I enjoy the taste of heaven immensely now. And better yet, I know perfectly well when I am moving away from heaven on earth and flirting with the neighborhood of darkness. What is the best way to use the law of attraction, and could I please copy and paste a couple million dollars?

"First of all, you must believe with all your being that the work you are doing is going to benefit humanity, whether you are selling apples, performing heart surgery, or being a light worker. You also need to learn to perform your mission from the love of your heart. Even if the working conditions are not yet to your total liking, do your work with complete love from your heart, with the knowledge that love can change the working circumstances in an instant. By sending out love frequencies to the universe, you will attract the right opportunities. Transform fear into love to start the changes that you desire in your life. Also, your connection to the divine has to be clear, and your mind needs to be at peace. Clear communication comes from a mind at peace, a heart flowing with love, and a joyful attitude. Clear signals produce great results."

To attract what we desire, we operate from love and learn the best divine technology to maximize our copy and paste command. Do I get this right?

"That is correct. When your heart is in the love frequency and you have cleared your communication pathways, you can access the correct guidance. Creation is always flowing; therefore, you must direct the flow for your highest good and the good of humanity."

In other words, if we have a thinking problem, we will still create but not exactly what we need or want or what is best for humanity. Am I on the right track?

"You are on the right track, my dear. War and mistreatment of other humans are created out of thoughts of fear, greed, and hate. When thoughts are based on love, creations are just as powerful and work for the enhancement of life and well-being for all."

When Jesus said, "Seek first the kingdom of heaven and everything else will be added unto you," what did he really mean?

"He was advising humanity to seek within and find the love frequency in their hearts. By seeking within, you learn to quiet the unnecessary conversation of the mind. When you quiet the chatter of the mind, you are on your way to getting to know the real you and getting acquainted with the power that the Creator has bestowed upon everyone.

"When you get to know this silence, you have access to your subconscious mind, where all your communication towers reside. When you have access to your communication towers and know their operating and maintaining systems, you can communicate with the infinite universal mind where all creation takes place."

That sounds extremely interesting. In other words, learn to work the system and avoid unnecessary U-turns and dead ends. One of Jesus's teachings was that when two of us agree in prayer, his Father in heaven will listen. Was he talking about the above teaching of getting to our silence and learning how our communication towers work?

"It is good to get together with others in prayer or meditation. The energy produced in genuine groups is of immense healing and creative power. But you are also right about the personal teaching. When you quiet the conscious mind and learn to direct and program your subconscious mind, you are on the freeway to the infinite mind of creation.

"Let me take this opportunity to bring out another very important teaching.

He taught individual advancement with the ultimate goal being the benefit of all. In other words, when you access your own divinity, you are contributing also to the benefit of others by magnifying wisdom and love not only for yourself but for the highest good of the planet and others."

I see, my dear Lady. I think I understand. When one of us reaches the light, it becomes contagious, and it expands and adds to the reservoir of the planet's light, and that light is beneficial to every living thing. Now I understand the teaching that heaven rejoices when even one soul gets to salvation.

"You are getting there, my dear child. It is one for all and all for one. This is why it so important for awakened people not to get discouraged, because the unseen benefits of being light and teaching light can reach unimaginable corners of darkness and despair."

Thank you. This makes so much sense. I will do my best not to get discouraged and will keep in mind than even a kind word or a genuine smile can make a big difference in difficult situations. Now, could you explain to me where all these communication towers are and if mind is in every part of our being—or is mind the brain?

"Great question, my dear. I see you went for coffee already. Well, let's take it one step at a time. Your complete being is designed to work in total unison with the light. You have the potential for wisdom in every cell of your body. Your being should be as illuminated as the night sky with a multitude of stars. The secret is learning how to connect the light to all the receivers of the light. Do you understand, my child?"

I sure do. I'm on my third cup of coffee. So our subconscious mind has all this equipment and programs to help us access the wisdom that resides in the all-knowing mind of creation. To get to the subconscious, we train the conscious to shut up and listen. And when we have the mind static under control, we can reprogram our system.

"Good analogy, my child. By learning what Jesus thought, you go within, and you find inner silence and peace. When you are in silence and peace, you access the intuition switch that illuminates the wisdom pathways that lead to the Father or infinite mind of creation. When you arrive to this sacred space, you have mind, body, soul, and spirit performing a magical dance that can move any obstacle along your path. And this beautiful dance, my dear, is called heaven on earth.

"I know that all this information can be difficult to understand and put into words, and I wish to thank you for your sincere efforts and patience in understanding these teachings."

Don't worry. I will not quit this time. Patience has not been one of my virtues, but you have gently guided me and taught me the lessons, including patience with myself. I am also excited about uncovering all these teachings. I am tired of all those U-turns and dead ends.

"Please remember that getting to the light for most humans is a work in progress. It will be a daily decision to transform your thoughts of fear into thoughts of love. With consistency and the help from your guides and angels, the progress will be evident day by day. When you are consistent with your spiritual practices, the only option is success."

Thank you. I like that option. I know that it is a daily endeavor, especially if we are carrying wrong programs from our childhood and damaging viruses of the mind. But we will see progress if we are totally committed to advancement. I am optimistic, my Lady. Pray for me please. I need all the light you can spare.

Now getting back to the law of attraction, many people are trying every approach these days to maximize the law of attraction, but many are disappointed with the results. Would you say that in some cases they have to look at redoing their sacred contracts and looking into past-life connections?

"You are correct. You have to use your wisdom and become your own detective to figure out where the obstacles are placed. Healing is always possible, whether the obstacle is a creation from your present earth life, from an overly ambitious sacred contract, or from a past life. I am extremely proud of you for resolving the issue with your own experience of the repeating pattern with your soulmate from a less illuminated part of town."

Now you are making me laugh, calling hell a less illuminated part of town. So it does not matter how many vision boards we have or how many affirmations we repeat every day if we have a block stemming from those areas mentioned?

"It is still beneficial to go ahead and do those good things, but if the pattern is totally beyond your comprehension, you need to look deeper and carefully at every aspect in order to advance faster and joyfully."

How do we take better care of our bodies in order to be a better house for the spirit?

"By working diligently on your spiritual life, you are automatically working on your physical body. Spirit will be guiding you every step of the way as to the necessary changes in nutrition and well-being practices. I will give you three essential keys to help you in your overall process for attaining spiritual well-being: a sound mind and a strong body. Mastering your breath is essential in spiritual health. Daily prayer and meditation aid in mental health. A hydrated body is a steppingstone for physical health."

Thank you, my dear Lady. It makes total sense, and it seems so easy to implement those practices into a daily routine. And of course, I dance and practice yoga every day to maintain my joy.

We put all that together, and we have taken serious steps for our overall health.

I understand that some people are born already with a clear channel, and others need some tuning up. For those of us divinely challenged, how do we clear our channels and access divine wisdom?

"If your channel needs clearing, the best way to accomplish this is by developing your own practice of prayer, contemplation, meditation, or any other habit that can quiet the mind and exercise control of your thoughts.

"Always remember that the breath is life, and a good breathing practice is one of the keys to manifesting good health and happiness. You also need to stay in joy because depression is not conductive to manifesting the things that you desire."

You are so right. I have manifested some pretty shitty stuff when I have been sad or angry. Where are you guys when I am miscreating and messing up?

"In the same place of love, praying and waiting for you to learn the lessons from having walked away from joy. When you walk away from joy, you get into anxiety and despair. When you get into those states, you block your channels of communication because you are moving away from the light."

I understand your point, but sometimes my life becomes a wild party of misadventures. Within the span of a few years, I was hit with a divorce, the loss of great-paying job, and a difficult menopause. And if that was not enough, my teenagers were misbehaving, I met my soulmate from hell, and for the icing on the cake, Hurricane Katrina destroyed everything I owned. Tell me, what is a normal human being to do? My friends tell me that they would be on their third nervous breakdown by now. I probably had a few but was too busy to notice. My daughter tells me that I am already crazy but that I am smart enough to cover it up. She gets her sense of humor from her mother.

"My dear child, when you are presented with several events and lessons, the first thing to do is to find your love center again and ask for guidance. Please do not be tempted to get into the blaming game. Regain your sense of humor and find ways to be in joy.

"In your particular case, you knew very well that the marriage contract was nearing the end because you were advised so in your dreams. When it comes to marriage contracts, remember the other person has his or her own lessons to experience too. In the work situation, in reality, you were tired of doing the same thing for so many years, and you had signaled to us your desire for change. And my beloved teenagers have been misbehaving since the beginning of the world; that is part of their lessons and yours.

When it comes to natural disasters, they are part of the energy that moves the universe, and they have been happening since the beginning of our wonderful, mysterious universe."

Yes, but what about menopause? After all we do for creation, we get rewarded with a painful and depressing rite of passage. What kind of cosmic reward is that?

"You said the magic words, my dear. It is a rite of passage, and it should be a joyful one, not a painful and depressing one. If you prepare ahead of time, menopause does not have to be traumatic. It is actually a great time for rebirth and transformation. It is a time when you can give birth to new ideas and projects. You can form new friendships, and you can help in the education of younger generations. It is a time to share your wisdom with the world and help others find their inner light. Women should be given time and understanding during this process. By claiming your divine feminine rights, women will be changing rules and laws to assist them in this transition."

Please help us with these changes, dear Mother. After performing several jobs in and out of our homes, we usually end up working for pennies in our later years, when I believe our retirement benefits should start many years earlier than men's. After all, without our nurturing, they would not be the rulers of the world.

"Amen, my love. Heaven is working on that regard, and many of you are hearing our urgent call to unite and work in invoking the spirit of the Divine Feminine and invite this energy to multiply and spread her wisdom and love to every corner of the world."

Thank you for your prayers and urgent calls, my dear Mother. I know that some of us are listening because we are tired of the old system. Do you think that we are really capable of changing things on earth and creating a world where the power of love will be permanent for every human being?

"When more people start looking for the truth and make a decision to access their divinity, transformation on all levels will take place. The power of love is ready to take over the world, but humans have to make the decision to move from fear and hate to love and unity."

I think more of us are trying to awaken and start practicing love and unity principles. I have become aware of many groups getting together for prayer, meditation, and gatherings to support each other. We need all the assistance from heaven. What do you think of our efforts?

"Many blessings are created when people focus on raising their energy and forming groups for that purpose. We work alongside you when such benevolent work is initiated by humanity. Please do not become discouraged; even a few people gathered in the name of love and unity can make an immense difference in the shift for the entire planet."

That is very encouraging, dear Mother. I will keep doing my part and gathering with other sisters of like mind to keep the blessings flowing.

Please explain to me the fact that sometimes you say God, light, Spirit, divine wisdom, or the Father. Are these just different names for the same Creator or Source?

"I am so sorry if have confused you. Everything is oneness, my dear. The light is everything. Remember Jesus said you are the light of the world. If you are the light of the world, you are one with Spirit, divine wisdom, Creator, and so on. I give you the different names to make it easier for you to choose a name that would make you feel more comfortable and loved."

I am definitely making you work today. Thank you. It is totally clear to me now. Yes! I am divine, I am a goddess, and I love myself with all my heart, with all my soul, with my entire mind, and with all my strength.

"Well, my darling, you just came up with a perfect affirmation based on Mark 12:29–30. Keep up the good work."

Human Relations

I know that Jesus taught us to love our neighbors as we love ourselves. How can this be accomplished when there is so much separation and selfishness these days, even in the churches?

"If you pay attention to the complete teaching in Mark 12:29–34, he also said that the Lord our God is one Lord. And his instructions were to love thy God with all thy heart, with all thy soul, with your entire mind, and with all thy strength. When you learn the meaning of this gem of wisdom, you will have no problem with loving your neighbor as you love yourself and as you love the Creator."

I think I understand, dear Mother, why you are pretty much basing the awakening and transformation plan on this passage in Mark 12:29–34.

"I knew you were catching on. I am so impressed; you are paying attention. You are actually advancing by bigger steps now."

You probably thought I would never make that connection. But I am getting better at reading your messages. This passage of the Bible has been showing up in my life everywhere, and to understand this passage is to accelerate our way to embracing your teachings of heaven on earth. But anyway, you are not the only one impressed today that I am actually making sense this early in the morning. You know I am not a morning person, and I am not thrilled when you wake me up so early with your sweet commands to get up and write.

"Well, be careful what you pray for; you asked for an increase in your understanding of our love teachings, and you know that I love to teach."

I know that divine timing is better than my timing. I just wish that your timing could be more like 9:00 a.m. and not 3:00 a.m.

Since I am on a roll this morning, let's see if I can put my conclusions into words. When Jesus says the Lord our God is one God, I believe he is speaking of the unity of everything. Divine light is one with us, and we are that—pure light. Therefore, we are in unity with this force that creates everything. This is the blissful oneness that I experienced the night my friend kept her promise and came to visit me in the hospital.

Jesus was not speaking about a mean God, all-powerful up there in his throne, and us little, miserable sinners down here paving our way to hell with the sweat of our work. If God is one Lord and everybody and everything comes from the same source, we are also that source, and we are equipped with the same loving qualities of our Creator. If we love our Creator with all our heart, soul, mind, and strength, we are loving ourselves the same way because we are one with God. And when we love ourselves unconditionally and know that love permeates everything and everybody, we cannot help but love our neighbor as we love ourselves and as we love God. What do you think, my Lady?

"You have understood the essence of the teaching on love, my child. The Creator is infinite love, you are infinite love, and your neighbor is infinite love. When he teaches to love God with all your heart, soul, mind, and strength, it is totally for your own benefit. It is not God being selfish and forcing you to love and worship him. It is God asking you to recognize that you are divine and to love that divinity within every aspect of yourself. When you love your own divinity, you are in unity with infinite love, and you will have compassion for those who are operating from a center of hate and confusion instead of love.

"You will be quick to forgive because you know that they do not know what they are doing. Your heart will be eager to send them all the love possible for their prompt healing. Once you understand the teaching that creation is all about love, you will have love for your neighbors even if you disagree with their actions."

I see. This is the cry of Jesus on the cross of "Father, forgive them because they know not what they do." He knew that by hurting him, they were hurting themselves and taking giant steps backward on their awakening road. How sad that we think that we are winning by killing others.

I am practicing and working on understanding your loving approach, but I still get angry at petty things sometimes. I want to practice love but don't like being taken for a doormat. How do I scream with love and compassion?

"Jesus is infinite love, but he corrected injustices during his mission on earth. You are within your right as a visitor of earth to ask for respect for yourself and your hostess, Mother Earth. As a spiritual being, you exercise that right from your love center with wisdom, strength, and clarity.

"The minute you walk away from love, you are magnifying the opposite of love, and that is not beneficial for you, your neighbors, or creation.

"You are on your way to understanding and enjoying the journey. You learn daily from the happy and unhappy lessons, but both aspects are necessary in advancing toward the light. Please make sure to balance the world's way of doing things with the light's way of doing things."

I get it, Mother. Thank you.

If we are one with the Creator, why are we so imperfect? Shouldn't we be like little gods running around happily loving and caring for one another?

"That is the ultimate goal, to transform fear and hate into love and compassion. When you decide to put on the physical body, you know that the risk is great for forgetting your divinity and getting attached to suffering, but you also know that the rewards can be just as great and can translate into much-needed accomplishments for humanity."

Do you and Jesus think that you pretty much wasted your time coming on your rescue mission?

"Creation has a season and a reason for everything. The mission was taken at the exact time needed. The seed was planted, but like everything else in creation, it had to be in darkness for a while to become a great light. The teachings are finally being understood, and the light will shine as was originally intended."

I see your point. Even though his teachings are being taught everywhere and pretty much misunderstood, the mysteries are just beginning to be revealed, and the light workers are being prepared to teach others. I am excited. I can see the torch being passed from individual to individual for the enlightenment of the entire planet. We are getting ready for the Olympics of ascension. I love it. Hand us the torch, dear Mother.

"You do not cease to impress me, my child. The awakening of humanity is imminent, and the light workers are eager to carry the torch. Heaven is rejoicing."

Why were humans created in so many different looks, races, et cetera, and why do we look at our differences so much?

"Diversity is meant to be enjoyable. Once you awaken and realize that you are unified by the light, you are operating from a center of love.

When you are centered on love, you have no fear of diversity. You see other religious, traditions, or races as part of the grand divine plan."

If we all realized that we all come from love and light, we would not be dealing with the messes that we have created?

"That is correct. There would be no anxiety over your differences. When you think that you are separate from the divine and from everything else, you live in a permanent state of fear. When you reach the light, you understand that every human being has that spark of divinity within."

So our differences are not that great when we know that we all contain the same light and that this light comes from the same source. In other words, our vehicle might be different, but it is run by the same fuel. It is mind-boggling to think of billions of humans, all similar but completely unique. How is that even possible?

"It is a mystery worth studying, my dear. If everyone understood the miracle of life and appreciated the beauty and wonder of each individual, there would be no more violence in any shape or form on the wonderful planet Earth. The expression of love comes out uniquely, beautiful, and different every time, but the basic ingredient is from the same source and the same quality."

I had a great example of that teaching when my granddaughter was four years old. She loved M&Ms and did not like to share them. She would share everything else but not her adored "Nemanems," as she used to call them. She had just received a new bag of her favorite candy, and I asked her to give me a few pieces of her least favorite color. Her reply was "They are all my favorite colors because they are all sweet on the inside." What an insight from a child. The Creator loves our differences, and we should too, because our sweet source is the same, even if we arrive on earth with different coloring.

"We all delight in the wisdom of children. The love you are sharing with your granddaughter is being noticed in the heavenly realms, my dear. I kept reminding you that there were some nice rewards after menopause."

Thank you. That little angel has helped immensely in dealing with my health challenges and in finding my love center again.

How do we deal with the ending of a relationship or the unfair loss of a job without hating the people involved?

"There will be times in everyone's life when the universe will give you the opportunity for designing your life again. In other words, the door is open for undoing old contracts and creating new ones. Please do not overanalyze the event and do not create the belief that it is the end of the world or that the Creator is out to punish you. It is divine wisdom using divine timing and giving you strong encouragement to act and to see the opportunities that you can create from being fired or being left alone by a companion. Also remember that in some part of your desires program, you have placed a request for change and have advertised your request to the universe for the desired change. This is why I always remind you to be careful about your desires and prayers. Your words and thoughts are powerful commandments to creation.

"When you are experiencing a major change in your life, get quickly back to your love center. Be compassionate with yourself and those involved in the situation. If necessary, repeat the transformation plan to help you get centered and focused. Tell yourself that this could be the chance of a lifetime to prove that you are just as capable of creating as the person who just fired you. Motivate yourself to take the next step and to be aware of new opportunities. Make a plan and ask your guides to align your human plan to your divine plan. Remind yourself that creation is never-ending and that you are always ready to learn and contribute."

These days, relationships are started and ended in the public eye. Let's say a relationship is terminated and announced to the world. How do we get over the humiliation when it has been posted on the social networks? And do we have the right to humiliate that jerk back?

"First of all, that so-called jerk is also a spark of divinity who has not remembered yet his origins of love and light. Take it as an opportunity to strengthen your character. Do not answer in the same manner. Acknowledge the ending of the relationship and release it with love and peace. Results are always better when you act from your love center.

"Look for the lesson in the experience, yours and his, and ask your guides to help both of you learn the lessons. You might be the last person he hurts on his way to evolving, and that would be great for his confused soul and for your peace of mind. Please do not transform the love you have for him into hate because that would be a step backward on your ascension process. Undo the sacred contract you had with him and create a new, loving contract for your own benefit and for the expansion of light."

In other words, if I am on my way to enlightenment, I accept that I was part of his evolution and that he was part of mine, and do I have your permission to look for another jerk?

"After you go through the process of undoing and creating new contracts, and before you find another companion, take time to breathe, my child. Take time for yourself and ask for guidance. Get to know yourself. Be clear in what it is that you desire in a companion. Work on your talents and enjoy your own being, your family, your friends, and nature. Learn to love and pamper yourself.

"Do something that will enhance your life and the life of others, and the universe will take notice and will cooperate in helping you line up a compatible companion. When you are centered in love and wisdom, you can attract the companion who will add to your happiness, not subtract from it."

What about dealing with difficult people? My first impulse is to retaliate and give them a taste of their own medicine.

"You know the answer to that. You do not take their offenses personally. If they have the need to offend others, the problem is within themselves. They do not remember their own loving nature. Pray for them and send them love and believe that they will eventually discover their way to the light."

What is the best way to deal with a difficult person, especially family members? When conflicts arise, I usually just stay away and give no explanation.

"Yes, I know your way, my dear. It is an option, but it is not the most compassionate. The best way is to state your grievances clearly and explain to them that you want them in your life but will not stand for conflict. See them as struggling with their own evolution and not being centered in love. Accept them as they are and love them anyway, knowing that they are ascending at their own pace. If you are truly grounded and evolving, it is not a difficult proposition."

That's easy for you to say. I bet the angels never give you any trouble. So am I advancing my growth by putting up with idiots?

"You advance if you conquer the issue, but if you enjoy discussing the same grievances, you are just spinning your wheels and magnifying fear instead of love. With this approach, the lesson eventually shows up again, sometimes with the same person and sometimes with others.

"However, let me make one teaching clear. You need to keep in mind that sometimes friendships and relationships have to come to an end for the growth of every person involved. Even if you do not undo the sacred contract, some contracts run their courses naturally."

Okay, I think I get it. So the people who show up in our lives are part of our sacred contract when we come to earth. Some contracts have expiration dates and die of natural causes. However, we also have the right to undo contracts that are making life miserable for us. Is this correct?

"You are on your way to understanding this teaching, my dear. I know you love decorating. Think of living in the same house for several years with the same colors and furniture. From time to time, you love to bring in new colors and more beautiful things. You go about planning and designing with love and enthusiasm. You lovingly give away your old possessions to someone in need, and you bring your new possessions in. The entire process is one of excitement and joy."

That is a beautiful comparison, my dear Lady. Just as we can redesign our homes, we can redesign our lives. I know when I decorate, I am in my love center, and the ideas flow nonstop. If I need to redesign my life, I use the same approach. I lovingly let go of people and places that no longer fit in my new life, and I welcome new people, places, and experiences into my updated décor. No need for fights, hate, or fear, just letting go with love and compassion.

I now understand the above teaching perfectly, but what about impossible parents, siblings, and children?

"In that case, you have to do your best to honor the sacred agreement that you chose before arriving on earth. Feel gratitude for the lessons, whether you like the lessons or not. Give the situation your best effort, leaving no room for judgment and angry emotions. And always remember, every issue you conquer advances your path to enlightenment."

Can we undo a contract with a parent or a child?

"Let's go back to the decorating analogy; just as you can overhaul your entire house, sometimes just a few changes in color or lighting can make a huge difference. In the case of parents and children, the sacred contract stays in place, but you can make changes and rearrange little corners where you can bring in more light or flowers."

I like that. If I am the decorator, I should know how to make these changes and make the home more beautiful and inviting, and if I am a light worker, I should know how to make changes in our sacred contracts and make the situation bearable and maybe even enjoyable.

"I am so honored to be your guide. You have learned the teaching. I knew that I could get this to sink in with the decorating topic. I know that you can stay up all night changing a room, with no complains, may I add."

You are so right. I don't even miss my precious sleep when I am developing a new decorating idea. Please give me some advice on recreating our sacred contracts.

"When you decide to recreate your sacred contract, ask for divine assistance in making the necessary changes to the old agreement. Visualize the best result possible for the people involved in the sacred contract, and during meditation, imagine making the changes in the Sacred Book of Contracts. Heaven is delighted in assisting you with your new redesigning plans."

That sounds good to me. It is similar as to when a sports figure or a celebrity decides that the old working contract is not living up to their new image. They renegotiate with an expert's assistance, and it usually works out for the benefit of all involved.

Sometimes we get caught between feuding siblings or friends. What can we do to help others understand the teaching of learning to love like the Creator loves us?

"The ones who understand the way of the light can be of great assistance by listening and guiding them toward their own light. Pray and send love to all involved. Keep yourself centered in love without taking sides or sharing opinions. Know that this is their own learning experience, and your only contribution should be listening with compassion and love and praying for their own enlightenment."

What is the best way to teach others to find common ground?

"By example, show your own light, that you may clear the way for others. Gather with other people who are also working on the enhancement of life and appreciation of diversity."

But my light sometimes runs out of batteries. How do I keep my light shining bright?

"It runs out when you neglect your spiritual work or you let a less evolved brother or sister interfere with your peace of mind. If you see the difficult situation as a learning experience and take time to breathe before responding, the outcome should be beneficial to all the individuals involved."

I have meditated and sought the light for years, but some people still get to me. What is wrong with me? Is there hope for my enlightenment?

"You are advancing, my child. Have you noticed that what used to take years or months to process in your forgiveness program only takes a few hours or a few days now?"

Yes, I have noticed that hurts, or perceived hurts, do not bother me that much anymore. I try not to take things personally and remind myself that we are all traveling through this world at our own ascension pace. And you know this is a major accomplishment for me because my Latin temper and my Sagittarius nature can get the best of me at times.

"You are on your way, my child. Keep up the good work and evolve daily."

Thank you. You have noticed. I couldn't have done it without you patiently teaching me the way of the light with so much love and compassion.

LET'S TALK ABOUT MONEY

Many of us light workers have spent our lifetimes in spiritual pursuits and at times have neglected the financial aspect of life. Many of us think that money and spirituality do not mix. How do we combine both aspects and have peace and contentment?

"People forget that money is the tangible measurement for what you choose to create. Some light workers are afraid that by having money, they will lose their spirituality. When you understand that the marriage of heaven and earth includes prosperity, you have no blocks against abundance of money."

What is the best way to understand this teaching? How do we open ourselves to allowing abundance of money while maintaining balance in our lives?

"After the awakening plan, all these things become easier to handle. You will fall in love with the idea of creating good for humanity and in return creating abundance for yourself. Tell yourself powerful statements about money always. Know that money in your hands means goodness for yourself and others. Pray that others will understand this truth also.

"Money is a means to achieving your freedom and helping others achieve theirs. What people make with money is what becomes problematic. You should use money to be free to follow your dreams. Money is part of the energy that keeps the world moving constantly."

I know plenty of people who became greedy after beginning to make money, and accumulation of money has become their priority. How do we maintain the balance of having money without becoming greedy?

"Money is a powerful energy, and the secret in handling money is knowing that it has to flow always, just as the energy of love is ever flowing. And just like love, you never deplete your own reservoir if you learn how to manage the inflow and outflow of money. Nonattachment is essential in living life to the fullest. If you draw your security from money, a home, or another human being, you will eventually experience disappointment."

How do we learn to manage the inflow and outflow of money without getting overwhelmed by the task?

"This is a part of life where the combination of spirit and matter becomes critical. When Jesus said, "Be in the world but not of the world," he meant to learn the ways of the world but to know always that your main substance is spirit. In other words, learn how to manage your money as the experts of the world do it. And learn how to use your money as the experts of heaven would do it."

My head is spinning, but I think I can make some sense of what you are telling me. We do what we need to do to educate ourselves on how the experts create, manage, and invest their money. And to create harmony, we also learn from our heavenly family as how to best use our money for the enhancement of our lives and the lives of others.

"There is plenty of help in the world system to become an expert of your money management. And have you noticed that there is also plenty of help in the Bible? Jesus spoke of money management at all times. If you take advantage of all the assistance provided, then your money problems are a thing of the past. Please remember that money is not the problem. It is thinking that money is your security where the problem lies. There are many wealthy people who think they have money problems, but there are also people with very little money who think that life is an incredible adventure, and they do not have a problem in the world."

So would you say that we treat money like we treat a person we love?

"That would be a good start. Treat the flow of money in your life with love, dignity, and respect. Be grateful for the comforts that money can buy. Bless your money when it comes in and when it goes out. Bless the money you keep for your savings and bless the money that goes out to pay the expenses that keep your home in comfort. Always have a savings plan, even if it just a minimum amount; this is part of mastering the flow of money. Pick an organization that you know does good works and direct some of the flow their way monthly. Even a small amount flowing constantly will bring back an increase of your money flow. Help with your time also. Please remember time from a loving volunteer is worth plenty. Mentoring others is a blessing that will come back to you multiplied many times.

"Please do not develop feelings of insecurity when you pay your expenses or make your purchases. Be grateful that you are in the flow.

Know that the flow of money keeps people employed and families thriving. Send your money out with love and blessings and be in the knowing that it is coming back to you with love and blessings also."

Do you think that we are experiencing an epidemic of greed and insecurity?

We are in a world at the moment where the rich get richer and the poor get poorer. It seems that big-time bankers and corporation managers have an insatiable appetite for accumulating money or numbers representing money on computers and paper. The few honest politicians left are powerless against the powerful rich. How many millions do they need in the bank to feel secure? Even some light workers seem to be going this way. What can we do to save ourselves?

"As I have told you before, just as love is magnified with practice, so are fear and anxiety. Fearful human nature has been the same always, to accumulate in order to feel safe. You need to feel safe in your spirituality in order to avoid epidemics of this proportion. In these days of fast communications, it is easier for any type of energy to spread like a contagious disease or a wildfire. The flow of money has been seriously damaged by individuals lost in greed and selfishness. This energy is being magnified and spread daily."

So you do agree that it is reaching epidemic proportions? What can we do to stop what seems to me an incurable disease of greed? Will the energy of greed get so big that we are doomed to total collapse, which will force us to start over again?

"You know that change is constant and that sometimes the lessons have to be learned the hard way."

Are we headed for a major depression? Are we too late for a cure? I don't want another experience like Hurricane Katrina.

"First of all, light workers have to keep up their energy work and get more people involved in the way of the light. You must mitigate the effects of greed and fear by the more powerful effects of love and spiritual strength.

"It is in the people's hands to change the system. Activate the light in yourself and help others activate theirs. Become aware of corruption and negative practices and take action in demanding change. Work for harmony and integrity. Pray for middle ground; extreme and outdated ideas are one of the main problems of the economic and social systems of the world. Pray and meditate that healing takes place in the minds of greedy human beings and that the joy of sharing is restored for the benefit of all.

Major changes will take place when more people become aware that it requires unity and prayer to manifest changes for the overall improvement of any situation. Pray for this awareness to invade the world."

It seems like an impossible task to me, dear Mother, but I will do my share and trust that the solutions are coming.

"It is not impossible, my dear. Please keep up a good attitude and, yes, do your share; we are extremely grateful for that. It is from individual efforts that the chain reaction gets started."

I gather that the best way to make our living is to understand our mission and love our work. Most of us dream of freedom and creating from love, but plenty of people are barely surviving these days. What do we do if we are stuck in a dead-end job?

"Once you are on your way to enlightenment, even if you are not in your dream environment, you will be content and excited for the new possibilities. You will see your employment as a blessing for having been with you during your awakening process. The more you embrace gratitude, the sooner new doors will open up for you. Be diligent in your search for new opportunities and ask for guidance from your divine family. Maintain your joy and see the beauty in life daily.

"Please also realize that financial security is not the same for everybody. Some light workers might be content with a steady paycheck and some free time for their spiritual adventures, but others might need to start using their spirituality to create a new way of making a living. Whatever way is chosen, you are lovingly encouraged and gratefully acknowledged. We will be helping all along no matter what your desire might be. Step by step, you will accomplish it as long as you stay focused and divinely connected.

"Once you have left fear behind, you have raised your vibrations and you are operating from a higher state of being, where you create from love, not from greed or fear of poverty. When you are in balance, creation is easier and fulfilling. Do your power statements daily, such as these:

"Money empowers me to help myself and help others.

"I honor and love myself for creating and maintaining the flow of money.

"Be creative with your power statements and work on feeling abundant even if the actual cash has not arrived yet. When going for a walk, enjoy the scenery; it was created for your enjoyment. Feel thankful for the sunshine, the rain, the flowers, and so on. Enjoy a cup of coffee with a friend, or write a note to a distant friend or relative. Nature and friendships are priceless and yours to enjoy anytime you want.

"As you start enjoying the things that cannot be bought or sold, you will get used to the feeling of abundance. Please do not compare your situation with others. Everyone has their own path to follow. Keep in mind that at the right time, your abundance, materially and spiritually, is being revealed to you."

Jesus preached a lot about money, but he did not seem worried about his own finances. What was his real take on money?

"He lived in spiritual abundance and perfect joy, with no thoughts of lack or fear. He trusted that all his needs would be met because he knew his divine plan. He was instructing humanity in total salvation, and that meant financial salvation also."

So it is good to have money as long as we understand its power?

"It is great to have money. The mistake is in thinking that you have acquired everything on your own and forgetting that along the way, you had guiding angels on both realities. When you are creating from the light, you are eager to give and to teach others the way.

"If you make attachments your priority, then you are sailing away from the light. When you are grateful for your accomplishments and are generous with your money, your mission is enjoyable and stays crystal clear. You create the heavenly path of receiving and giving."

Is it okay to shop and enjoy beautiful things?

"Sure it is. Those beautiful things are someone's creation. Respect and bless their creations so others can do the same to yours. Make sure that you do not get your sense of security from earthly possessions. If you are grounded in your spirituality, you have joy with things and without things."

Tell me about it. I have lost my beautiful possessions several times now. So I have learned to enjoy what I have, without becoming attached to stuff.

How do we balance and limit our consumption to help preserve our beautiful planet?

"By understanding that beautiful things are like vitamins to your existence, but even vitamins in excess can be toxic."

So the magic word is moderation in everything we do?

"That is correct. Excess acquiring will keep you from your spiritual practices and puts unnecessary burdens on Mother Earth. When you are ready for new and beautiful creations, make sure to help others with your discarded ones. Do not accumulate in excess; keep the flow going in the love circle of receiving and giving."

Would you agree, dear Mother, that we even have to use moderation with our spiritual practice?

"Yes, my dear. Real success is to know the balance between spirit and material planes. Make time for your practice daily, even if is just a few minutes. Remember that the best practice of all is to be in gratitude always and realize that meditating and praying can be incorporated in every activity just by practicing gratitude and admiring the wonder and magic of life."

When we are in gratitude and make life a never-ending prayer, the flow of money becomes easier?

"You are on your way to understanding this lesson. The more you understand that life is not meant to be a constant struggle, abundance in every sense of the word will begin its magical flow. Jesus never preached poverty; his teachings have been manipulated and misunderstood. He advised to be aware of the darkness that can come when you acquire and hoard just for the love of power. He was against using money to humiliate and dominate others. As I told you before, he had riches at his disposal from his divine connections and from human connections."

I now understand that the best way to make our living is to understand our mission and love our work.

"That is correct. When you are aligned with creation, your mission is revealed to you, and when you possess that revelation, earning a living becomes a joyful journey of receiving and giving. Allowing the light to inspire you makes the path to abundance enjoyable and satisfying."

I have heard teachings that the way to heaven is narrow and painful. But now I understand that heaven does not need a life of sacrifice from us. Am I correct?

"Run as fast as you can when you hear such nonsense. Heaven wishes for you the very best always. And never forget that there is infinite help at your disposal. Ask for help with your divine plan and visualize your goals and dreams during meditation. Please make sure to get acquainted with the feeling of gratitude at every step of your abundance ladder."

Let me ask one final question for this section, dear Mother. I have noticed that you always mention the action of receiving and giving. But we have been taught that it is better to give than to receive.

"As you would say, you are on a roll today. I am so impressed that you have noticed. Remember that the story of my son's life was taken over by men. I have one little, important mystery for you: men give and then receive. For women, it works the other way around. You receive and then give."

Now you are on a roll, my dear Lady. This makes total sense in every aspect of our lives. Starting with conception, we receive and then we give to the world the new miracle of life. It is the same with Mother Earth; she receives when we plant, and then she gives us her wonderful gifts to nourish our bodies.

When I receive respect and attention, I love to return the same. But be afraid of my giving if I receive mistreatment and abuse. The abuse will be returned to the sender along with a few flying cooking utensils. But seriously, I think that we women have the power to multiply and share everything good we receive. Men, be smart and keep all those nice presents coming; heaven loves you for that. I shall get used to the new way, and I totally like it. I just made up my new mantra: I love to receive, so I can give.

Thank you, my Lady. We had a very good session today.

THOUGHTS ON HEALING

Let's talk about healing. Why it is so difficult to heal ourselves? I have practiced Mayan energy healing, healing touch, and other healing methods for years, and I have had more success helping others to heal than with my own healing. It is very frustrating to know that I can help others but have difficulties healing myself.

"Going back to the teaching on receiving, you also need to know that you deserve to receive your own healing. It is beautiful to help others, but you must know without a shadow of a doubt that your own healing is just as important as the healing of others. Sometimes the healing will come from your own methods, but be prompt in asking for help and receive the blessings from other healers or the medical profession.

"Healing is just another form of creation. People have been programmed to think that healing is outside the body, when in reality, the body is equipped with everything needed for healing. When you seek within, you realize that you are capable of reaching that part of divine intelligence that has the answers to your health challenges, as well as any other life challenge. Always remember that you are the instrument to be used for the light of healing, and it is imperative that a healer keeps her being finely tuned. Once you understand this truth, you will know when to help others and when to withdraw and totally help yourself.

"When healing does not take place, do not think that it is some kind of punishment. It is simply not aligned with that part of you that produces health and well-being. If death comes, spirit simply put an end to the struggle. When there is disharmony, spirit always takes the lead to end the suffering."

That is a powerful statement and good to know.

I spent over a year healing from stomach problems that are too numerous to list. What was this all about, and did I miss the signs from my guides?

"You are a special child, my love. A part of you did not want to admit that you were again looking for radical change. You knew that there were many things that you needed to change in your personal and professional life. You felt guilty about these changes because you thought that sacrifice was the way to salvation. And let me remind you that you had also neglected your spiritual practice.

"Then between the stress of making a decision and your fear of change, you reached access to that part of you capable of manifesting a mysterious disease of your digestive system. You knew you were playing with fire because you know exactly how the body's energy centers function."

You are so right. I literally felt that my stomach was burning. I wanted change, but I was afraid to make the move. And because I did not ask for divine guidance when I made the move, I chose the wrong door. And the prize behind this door was the lesson that I should have learned years ago, which is described in the chapter "My Soulmate from Hell."

A friend once told me that I was more afraid of success than of failure, and I think that this fact is true for many people. We know that life is always changing anyway, and to get different results, we must try different things. Why are we so afraid of change and success?

"That is correct for many people because success means giving up your time and privacy, and success carries plenty of responsibilities with it. Others are reluctant to show the world their greatness for fear of criticism or judgment."

In other words, in order to keep ourselves from success, we avoid change, and then we convince ourselves that we are comfortable hiding from the world and that we were born for the same old routine.

What are the signs to look for when change is totally necessary in our lives?

"Now let me make one thing perfectly clear. There are souls that come to earth to experience a more structured life and a routine that changes very little. If you are content with that experience, you are fulfilling your sacred agreement, and your light is still shining bright. But if you feel that you don't belong and your soul is yearning to sing, then you are destined for something greater than what you are experiencing at the moment. It is your right to ask for guidance in creating a more fulfilling and different life."

I see what you mean. In one of my traveling adventures, I stayed for six weeks with a family in Costa Rica. The lady of the house was without a doubt one of the brightest lights that I have encountered in my life. She did not have the yearning to see the world or to travel much, but she was wise beyond belief, even though she had only finished the sixth grade. She woke up singing every day, and the highlight of her day was daily Mass and treating her guests with love and joy. Her happiness was contagious, and her love for humanity was immense. Her entire day was a complete spiritual practice sharing faith, love, and joy. I would wake up listening to her beautiful voice singing to the new morning with gratitude and pure joy. I cherished those days spent with this beautiful lady for the many lessons in love and compassion that she so lovingly taught me. She has made her transition now, but her lessons will live in me always, and in my opinion, she was the ultimate guru. Her light shines in me and I am sure in many other people who were lucky enough to be her guests at her loving home. Her legacy to her family is immense love and faith.

"I know, my dear. You were witness to a wonderful example of someone whose light shines bright by just being humble and sharing from the love of her heart."

Let's get back to my struggle with all those ailments. Did I miss the signals?

"We are always alerting you. We did send you the necessary messages or roadblocks when you were about to embark on another round of that same lesson that you refused to untangle previously. The messages were there for you, even before you met your soulmate for the first time."

Oh, dear Mother, I think I could write several books from that repeating pattern of my life. I knew that in order to grow, I had to take a big leap, but deep within me, I was still afraid of change, and to avoid change, I decided to repeat a pattern that I knew would keep me stuck in the mud of hell. This confused my poor body, and it reacted with unexplainable ailments and a refusal to heal.

"However, my dear, after the mud came the refreshing, clean water and the understanding that you needed to invest your energies in undoing the repeating pattern, and when you asked for help, the assistance was immediately available. You know exactly how your being operates. You were on one of your learning adventures. But let's look at the good that came from it. You had time to map out your next step and to finally get your journals in order and start writing this book. You also took care of family matters and enjoyed your own company. When you were ready to heal and ask for help, all the assistance was lined up for your recovery in every sense of the word. You were treated by compassionate doctors and healers and began to trust your own inner guidance for your overall well-being."

You are so right. In my prayers, I asked for a female doctor who could spend time listening to my long list of ailments. And I can say that I met the best nurse practitioner in the world, who gently guided me through the entire medical process. At every step of the process, the person I needed at the time offered help. I have also learned a lot about the inner workings of my body while practicing self-healing techniques.

I was also able to help my son with his recovery after the vicious attack that he suffered. I have to thank you for helping us when we needed you the most with his healing. May I tell the story, and hopefully we can help others heal and recover from similar incidents?

"Be my guest. I was so proud of you for listening and facilitating the healing."

I still get sad when I remember that beautiful summer day when I went to bed happy, grateful for a pleasant and peaceful day. Little did I know that things were about to change.

I was awakened early in the morning by a knock at my door from my son's girlfriend (at the time), and I knew instantly that this could only be bad news.

My son and one of his friends were in the hospital after a brutal beating leaving a nightclub. On my way to the hospital, I kept arguing with you for not protecting my child. I was ready to fire my team of protection angels.

When I saw my son at the hospital, I had to use every ounce of strength to look at his bloody and swollen face and his pride in complete shambles.

The doctor told me that it was imperative to schedule emergency surgery as soon as the swelling went down to repair his broken face. She also added, "If he sneezes, he will be in danger of popping one of his eyes out because his face bones are fractured in several places." They also stated that he would be facing several cosmetic surgeries down the road.

I told myself, *We will follow the doctor's instructions*, and even though I was upset with my team of protection angels, I would still ask for divine help. Riding back home, I was still arguing with you, but what you told me next totally assured me that everything happens for a reason. You stated that eventually I would see the good of all this and that my son had just learned a big lesson, even if it would take him a long time to assimilate the entire lesson.

He had been hit on the back of his head, fell to the concrete, and lost consciousness. While he was lying on the concrete, his perpetrators kicked him mercilessly and shattered his face. As we left the hospital, I was thinking that in a fair fight, my son would fight to the bitter end. What you told me next took my breath away. You said, "Listen to your own thought. Your son is capable of fighting until the bitter end." And then the realization hit me, that it could have been a major tragedy, and that it was better to deal with doctors and hospital paperwork instead of funeral homes or attorneys' offices. After our conversation, I felt somewhat peaceful and started planning my son's healing with heavenly help.

After we got home, I followed the doctor's instructions and let him rest. Later that day, I asked my son's permission to do an energy healing session.

Before a treatment, it is my normal practice to ask you, dear Mother, and Jesus to please be present and to use me as an instrument for healing. I also thank you both ahead of time for the healing that is about to take place. But what happened next totally shocked my every cell. As soon as I felt Jesus's presence, I told him, "This one is in your court. I will owe you big-time."

To my total surprise, he told me, "Forgive the perpetrators, and then we will get started."

I was about to protest and give up, and you, dear Mother, told me, "Remember the first miracle. Follow his instructions." I was desperate for my son's healing, and I prayed and sent love and light to the other young men. I also asked their higher selves to please start working on compassion for others.

I felt the peace of forgiveness immediately, and we began the treatment. After forgiving, I became totally cleared and connected to the Master's energy, and to this day, I can remember the sounds of my son's fractured bones going back in place and feeling totally suspended in another dimension. There was no doubt in my mind that healing had taken place. This was an uplifting feeling of knowing and trusting.

The doctor had told me that his face would get worse before it got better, but I refused to believe those words and affirmed for me and for my son that healing was ours for the asking. After the healing touch treatment, it took just a couple of days for the swelling to go down.

To everybody's surprise, when he went back for his checkup and to schedule surgery, we got the news that surgery would not be necessary, but I had known that all along.

I need to make something very clear. My son grew up believing in the "crazy alternative" methods of his mother, as his dad used to say. He had the privilege of having been healed of asthma by the natural remedies of my mother and grandmother. After I became a Reiki practitioner, any time my children felt sick, the normal order was "Mom, come Reiki me." Therefore, my son had total belief in the treatment. I had asked for divine help, and by forgiving and praying, I had cleared my communication channel for healing to take place.

I believe that in order to manifest healing, there are several components that have to be present: total faith that healing is possible, forgiveness, gratitude, and the main ingredient, love. At the moment of healing, my love for my son and for the presence of my divine guides was beyond measure, and my total focus was on divine results. My mind was overcome with faith, and my heart with love.

When I got sick in my gut from situations that I could not stomach anymore, I accessed the part of me that is capable of creating chaos. But in a different situation, where I felt love and gratitude, I was able to access and manifest healing for my son.

Why did you ask me to remember the first miracle and told me to do as he asked?

"Because I know that you love the mysteries of his miracles, and you would know immediately what I was talking about."

I was confused by your answer but quickly realized that the servants at the wedding in Cana must have been just as shocked when they were told to fill all those containers with water to be transformed into wine. He was asking me to transform my anger into forgiveness for the healing to take place.

"Exactly, my dear. As I told you before, some things are difficult to comprehend by the human mind. But when you trust in divine guidance, explanations are not necessary."

What are the steps to follow when we develop a disease and we need to manifest healing?

"Get quiet and review your forgiveness program. Tell your body that it needs to cooperate in its own healing process. Scan your body and ask yourself if you have been sharing space with disease-producing emotions. Look for emotions of anger, fear, resentments, or heavy burdens from the past. Seek medical help and do your best to align your health practitioner's advice with your own healing. And always ask for divine assistance. We are always ready to assist you and guide your steps to produce the best possible outcome."

Thank you, my Lady. I have learned to trust some doctors again, and now I realize that by combining their skills, divine guidance, and my alternative therapies, I have reached a balance between all systems for my highest good.

"There is wisdom and healing in the world's system, my child. And divine guidance is always available. Learn to work with your own body and take the best of both worlds."

How do we accept nonhealing and the death of a loved one?

"It is a human emotion to be sad, so please don't suppress it. Go through the grieving process and keep in mind that the soul was fulfilling its divine agreement. Nobody has punished you or the dear one who exited. Death is part of an elaborate plan for the continuity of the energy that sustains the planet.

"Also remember that your loved ones can hear you and will always be thinking of ways to communicate with you. Open your heart to such loving communication and keep in mind that spirit is eternal. They do their best to get your attention by any means possible, such as dreams or by sending little signs to remind you that their love is eternal and always flowing."

That is beautiful, dear Mother, but why do we have such a hard time accepting death?

"Because of the wrong idea that death is an ending, and fear of not knowing what happens after death. It is just a process required for being in human form. When you map your trip to earth, you are certain that you will enjoy the trip and also certain that you will enjoy your return to the spirit world."

And we are excited to have our round-trip tickets to earth?

"That is correct, my child. If you see life as a wonderful part of a huge, divine plan, you will enjoy your time on earth and feel blessed for the opportunity to contribute, and you will feel secured in the knowledge that love is never-ending. Always remember that you planned your trip to earth out of love, and you always return to unconditional love."

Emotional Healing

You know one of the most difficult lessons of my life was having been sexually abused as a young child and having been so scared of adults that I could not confide in anybody. I felt guilty about keeping quiet, but I also knew that I would feel devastated if I told and nobody believed me. I felt that everybody had let me down. I thought that my mother was too busy fixing other people's problems to care about mine, and my father was too busy drinking himself to death. I had been labeled a shy child, and most adults believed that label and would not engage me in conversation.

Unfortunately, at this time, I also blamed my heavenly family and decided to cut my direct communication with the heavenly realms. I became more withdrawn and kept to myself most of the time. I had many good friends, and I trained myself to listen to them but talked very little about myself. It became a pattern in my life; it seemed that everybody loved to confide in me, but I did not feel comfortable trusting anybody. It was easier helping others with their pain than dealing with my own.

"Now let's reverse roles and let me ask the questions for a while. How did you manage to forgive and go on with your joy of life?"

As you know, it was a long roller-coaster journey because I had put the hurt in a compartment that I thought was sealed forever. However, it would leak out periodically, and just when I thought I was over it, something would happen that would remind me of the little box in my mind that contained all those scary memories. I was very good at sealing the lid and keeping it closed for long periods of time, but my mind would play tricks on me once in a while, especially in times of stress, and remind me of the contents of my little box, torturing me with the memories.

By all accounts, I led a normal life. I had fun and enjoyed life as much as I could, but it was a struggle sometimes trying to keep that lid shut. When I knew that my marriage was beyond repair, I was so busy trying to keep my family life together that I did not have a lot of energy left to keep that box from spilling over. A few months after the separation, the nightmares began. I have always been proud of my dreams, because I can usually solve problems and get guidance through my dreams, but I was not prepared for this type of dreaming.

Every single night, I woke up sweating and crying from the exhaustion of the nightmare. The dream never changed. It would start with me taking a walk through a beautiful, sandy landscape and a peaceful ocean. Suddenly, the landscape would turn into a crazy obstacle course, and a dark graveyard would appear out of nowhere. I would run, desperately looking for the grave of the person who abused me. This person had been dead for many years.

I would run and fall and start running again and would see skulls scattered on the sand. I knew that the next grave would be his, but at that very instant, I would wake up crying. I could not get to the next step in the dream, and it was totally frustrating in the dream as well as in my daily life.

These nightmares went on for months until one day, I was driving to work, crossing a long bridge over the lake, when a huge panic attack showed up. I felt like I could not drive anymore, and as soon as I crossed the bridge, I parked my car and cried for what seemed like hours. It seemed like every toxic emotion and every bad experience from my entire life was showing up to torture me in that exact instant. I was in panic of going insane. My heart was pounding, my legs were shaking, and I was holding my breath.

"And did you remember to pray and ask for help, my dear child?"

After a long cry, I took control of my breath first. Then I yelled and cursed at everybody and everything. And finally, I prayed. I guess I had the steps in reverse; prayer should have been my first act after regaining control of my breath.

"And what happened after you prayed? Did you feel that we were there to comfort you?"

It made a major difference. I got quiet and decided to trust and listen. I felt surrounded by love and guidance and knew instantly that eventually all these experiences were going to be the steppingstones to a better life. I also felt guided to ask for help and to stop being superwoman. I turned around and went home, and then I called a lady I knew who did healing work with hypnosis. I explained to her what had just happened. She was very encouraging and compassionate, and she knew that I needed immediate help. She advised me to come over to her office right away, and she said,

"Sometimes we healers need help also." I had a metaphysical store at the time. We were doing several modalities of healing work, and I was teaching meditation and studying Reiki.

This was the beginning of my healing process. I was advised to keep a dream journal and to analyze the dream. Little by little, I realized that the dream was an alert, and it should not be scary to me because it was my reality that was terrifying. The dream was telling me to quit running and find a burying site for the pain. The beautiful landscape was my life before the abuse, and I desperately wanted to get back to that peace of mind and joy. The ocean was telling me to seek some healing waters to help me deal with the memory in my every cell. I could no longer confront the individual since he was dead, but I was alive, and I had the power to put an end to the nightmares. My new boyfriend, who had been puzzled by my sudden changes of mood and my crying marathons, was by now my confidant, and his presence was a great source of rest and at this difficult time.

After several sessions of hypnotherapy, prayer, and dream analysis, I woke up one morning elated that I had had a full night's sleep. Eventually, the nightmares were turned again into my beautiful, vivid dreams where I could get answers to many of my questions and enjoy the interaction with my heavenly buddies.

Step by step, I started the process of forgiveness. I had blamed God, blamed my parents for not protecting me, and even blamed myself.

"Why would you blame yourself, my dear child?"

For having kept that horrible secret hidden for all those years and not confronting this person before he died.

"When did you finally consider yourself healed?"

When I realized that I had the power within me to transform all that energy that I was giving to the memories into something life-changing. I also realized that I had given this person the right to keep on hurting me every day, and that was not going to be tolerated anymore.

I also learned that one of the most important things a human being can learn is forgiveness. It is one of the main secrets of a happy life. I told myself that I had nothing to do with the other person's wrongdoings. I must admit that my mother is a forgiving person, and she has never let an offense stick around for long. I had learned some of the forgiveness processes from her.

"And have you thanked and blessed your mother for the lessons learned?"

You know I have done that. She is exactly the mother I needed for this life's experience, I believe that she fulfilled her sacred contract with me to the last detail. I love her and bless her daily. And to this day, I am still learning from her inner strength and love of life.

"What would you say were your more important insights from this healing experience?"

After the nightmares stopped, I was contemplating life one day, and I could feel that every day, the pain felt more distant to me, and suddenly, a light went on in my head, and I said to myself, "It takes the same energy for a thought to go back into the past and dwell in misery as it takes to stay in the present and plan a better life." Learning to be in charge of my thoughts was a major insight, my dear Lady.

I also decided to start loving myself and to be more gentle and kind with my own being. After all, I deserved some pampering as a reward for having lived some difficult lessons. I started a practice of going for a full-body massage often and doing more of the things that bring me joy. Loving me was another major insight. And last but not least, I learned that prayer and meditation are major tools needed for navigating this adventure called life.

When I arrived at all those discoveries, forgiveness was automatic, effortless, and liberating. By controlling my thought life, loving myself, and keeping up my spiritual practice, I could actually feel compassion for the confused soul that had forgotten his divinity, as well as his mission to teach love, not fear.

Slowly, I developed my spiritual practice again, and I found my way back to you and Jesus. I recovered that peaceful feeling that I had as a child when I communicated with the heavenly realms. Thank you, my Lady, for your loving guidance and for your encouragement during difficult times.

"It is our privilege to help our beloved children. We delight in the progress we see and in the knowledge that when one human reaches the light, many others will benefit from the same miracle."

How can we better help the victims of abuse, especially child abuse?

"The first thing to realize is that everybody has their own unique timetable for arriving at forgiveness. You can provide support such as listening and guidance, but the work is their own. By being supportive and maintaining your own joy and compassion, you are helping plenty. Be alert to signs of progress or despair and reach always for divine and professional assistance."

I guess I must have signed up for some difficult lessons on forgiveness, because I have had many situations that have needed my forgiveness. I have graduated with great honors, and next time around, I will take no other assignment but that of a spoiled, rich socialite.

Why is child abuse so prevalent, and where are our guardian angels when this is happening to us?

"There are certain barriers that only humans can conquer, and like you said it beautifully before, humans are suffocating in the toxicity of their own misdeeds. This is why our cry for the Divine Feminine Spirit to heal the world is of the highest urgency. We have not abandoned you, but we need your assistance in awakening to your own Divine Feminine Spirit, to activate the energy of healing and love and to bring light to such darkness."

I think that the time has come to understand the gift of love that a child is and to devote all of our resources to protect their lives. Our present treatment of children decides the future of our world.

A BITCH NAMED KATRINA

Just when I thought that life had given me a reprieve, Hurricane Katrina showed up. I was just going along with my boring, little life in southeastern Louisiana, bitching about menopause and thinking that things were calm in my up-and-down life. "Hold that thought," said life. "The biggest bitch of all is coming your way."

With the warnings that a storm was coming, I took another trip out of town, packing lightly for what I thought was just a long weekend. I was so used to these trips that I only packed enough clothes for three days, a few keepsakes, the most important documents, and some family pictures.

I finished packing, but I still had doubts about if it was necessary to leave town. My children were following their dad, and that gave me peace of mind. After I finished packing, I went to bed, debating whether to leave in the morning or to stay and brave the storm.

My boyfriend had reinforced his supply of alcohol and had no opinion on the subject. I prayed for wisdom, and in the morning, I woke up crying, and a feeling of total sadness had invaded my heart and my home. My gut feeling, or what I call an email of the mind, urged me to get the heck out of town and to pack a few more valuables, but I was too sad to pack any more stuff. I knew that I was coming back to devastation and that the story had already been written. Life was about to shows us a huge lesson.

Most of my relatives were heading for different destinations, and we decided to leave at the last minute, with Memphis, Tennessee, in mind. Traffic was the beginning of the nightmare, and we spent hours just trying to leave our town. After stopping at every hotel on the road, we were finally able to find a room in Tuscaloosa, Alabama. We woke up on August 29 to total disbelief. The news was not encouraging at all. We bonded with all the other guests at the hotel, who were also fleeing the monster. Communication was minimal, and the stories kept getting more horrendous by the minute.

The rest is history. My peaceful town of Slidell, Louisiana, was hit by the eye of the storm, causing destruction beyond belief. After a week in Alabama, we decided to head back, ignoring the stories of shortages of gasoline and hazardous driving conditions due to fallen trees.

I found myself rebuilding my life again and helping those around me. It seemed that everyone close to me went into a depression right after Katrina or a few months later. I kept telling myself, "Get busy rebuilding your life and helping those around you, and later we will see about depression or a serious nervous breakdown."

I had to recover from losing my possessions twice within days. After inspecting the destruction on the lower section of my home, my niece and I worked for a few hours salvaging a few things that were not broken or buried in the mud. This proved to be a heartbreaking task, but we managed to recover a few keepsakes and brought them upstairs. I had moved a few months earlier to this small townhouse, after selling my condominium, which had flooded twice before. I was in the process of looking for a house in a higher section of town to avoid any more floods. As is the norm in my life, the unpredictable happened, and Ms. Katrina had other plans and many lessons in store for me.

An employee of the townhomes assured me that they were hiring security and that the remaining belongings would be safe. The upstairs section was in pretty good order, and I left thinking that I should be grateful because at least I had a half a house, while many others were not able to recover anything.

I got busy surviving day-to-day and trying to find a new place to live, which proved to be more difficult than digging in the mud for my lost belongings.

A few days later, I went back to my townhouse to retrieve some clothes, and to my surprise, the upstairs was totally trashed. Everything worth taking had been taken, including jewelry and the best of our clothes and shoes. My precious collection of *Gone with the Wind* items was nowhere to be seen, as well as other collections. This led me to believe that they were professional thieves because they left the least expensive clothes and costume jewelry. They were not content with just taking the best; they stepped on my bed with muddy shoes, probably looking for hiding places on my tall headboard. They also trashed my entire bathroom. They looked for valuables in every corner of our two-bedrooms upstairs.

As I witnessed this disastrous scene, I gave myself permission to go for that promised nervous breakdown or at least for a good cry. I sat down on the stairs and cried for a long time, yelling at heaven and earth. Exhausted from my angry performance, I went outside to my tiny backyard and pretty much collapsed on the ground. I was too angry to call on my heavenly friends, and my mind was busy looking for blame and regret.

Slowly, I relaxed by taking deep breaths and quietly began to pray. I could literally feel my pain and everybody's pain taking residence in my being. I also felt Mother Earth's pain, and a feeling of sisterhood came over me, knowing that our destruction was her destruction and we were suffering together. I kept meditating and praying among all this destruction, and I resolved to find some more inner strength and to rely on my knowledge of oneness and unity.

I don't know how long I lay on the ground, barely aware of other people going in and out of their own homes. I was making mental notes of my losses and figuring out what I would miss the most. I remember that my diaries and journals had been in boxes downstairs, and that's what I would miss the most. Those were my treasures containing the story of happy and unhappy times of my life, the birth of my children, as well as the struggles with my material and spiritual life.

I finally got up, thanking Mother Earth for being a witness to my anger and sadness, and I promised to be partners in our mutual healing. I called in my guides, and I promised them that I would keep up my spiritual practices to help myself and others. After I went back inside, I felt lighter and could actually feel glimpses of joy and optimism.

I went upstairs again to retrieve my purse when an email of the mind told me to check a drawer on my nightstand. What a pleasant surprise. In that drawer were two of my most important journals, including the one of my experience with my departed friend the night my son was born. I didn't remember putting those journals there, but by then, I was used to knowing that miracles could happen in the middle of immense tragedies. I was overjoyed and left my muddy apartment with a renewed sense of gratitude for the small miracles in my life.

I think I had a more difficult time recovering from the looting than from the actual flooding. I had lived through other floods before, and I knew my way around rebuilding, but I could not imagine anybody being so greedy or needy that they would resort to stealing people's salvaged belongings. Did they know that the last few days had been horrible for the people of the Gulf Coast? Did they even realize that many of us had spent days trying to communicate with other family members and friends who had been separated by the storm?

I took long walks through our devastated streets, ignoring the debris and horrible smells, thinking about the cruelty of humanity. What makes a human being think that it is normal to add suffering and take advantage of such horrible circumstances?

After several days of analyzing and contemplating the situation, I came to several insights. I realized that if that was their way of making money, then they had a long learning road ahead of them, and life was going to make sure that they learned their lessons. I also realized that I was not those possessions, and I decided to never become attached to any material thing again. I would enjoy beautiful things but would always remind myself to keep my spiritual blessings above anything than could break or be taken away by nature or humans.

I lived with relatives for three months, and at times there were thirty people in a three-bedroom, two-bath house. How I kept my sanity is beyond my comprehension. My trusted, daily glass of wine and an occasional shot of tequila helped me with the incredible task of starting all over again. By then, I was a pro at starting over, so one more time would not kill me, but hopefully it would make me stronger and wiser.

By that time, I was back on better terms with my heavenly buddies. I was wiser, and I was determined not to let negative thoughts invade my mind. I kept up with my prayers and tried to steal silent moments to meditate, but it was a major effort to keep myself from descending into darkness again. There were days when I thought I was using my last drop of faith and joy just to get up in the morning and face the mountain of obstacles to accomplish very little. I still had my days of arguing with Mother Mary, but by the end of the day, I could feel her healing presence surrounding me and encouraging me to get joyful and enjoy the small accomplishments and the company of my relatives.

I asked my heavenly friends daily to show me the lessons in all that destruction and to help me keep my sense of humor and compassion for myself and others. One of the lessons I learned is that no matter what surrounds me, if I keep my joy and peace, things eventually will work out. I also kept steering my mind away from the compounded losses and into my daily chore of rebuilding our lives.

I stayed at the home of one of my nieces, and I chose to see this time as an opportunity to get acquainted again with many of the people I love.

My older sister, who I adore, kept me company and always made sure that I was eating right. I am one of those lucky people who loses her appetite in times of stress, probably to concentrate on drawing from divine substance.

This beautiful sister had been like a mother to me. She was twelve years older than I was and always acted like a mother, not a sister. I am so grateful for the time spent with her because cancer took her life exactly two years after Katrina. When I look back at those precious moments with her, I find one of the lessons in the fact that in those days, we were suffering material discomfort, but we had each other, and that love bond was reinforced more than ever. I am happy that we made the most of those three months and that I had the chance to let her know how much she meant to me. We spent hours remembering our roots, watching soap operas, and laughing at the incredible turns that life takes. We also realized that anything is possible when love is present and guiding every minute of our lives.

I am also thankful that I had already worked my way out of the pain of childhood sexual abuse. I think Katrina would have been a bigger nightmare for me personally if I was still struggling with that mountain of pain from the past.

Another lesson that I love to share with others is to work on emotional pain as soon as possible. Do not carry such big burdens for decades. They get heavier and heavier with the passage of time. And if you get blindsided by consecutives tragedies, it becomes more difficult to dig yourself out of it. Look for help—and the sooner, the better. There will always be a professional ready to help. Admit that you need help and pray or meditate for the right expert to guide you on your recovery. Ask the angels to assist you and talk to friends or relatives, and the answers will show up for your healing.

Even if you are a healer, there are things that require other people's insights and caring. Don't carry the burden alone; let others help.

By the time Katrina hit my life, I was somewhat used to asking for help. I had been little Miss Perfect most of my life and liked to assume the role of superwoman and protect everybody, but I was on my way to learning my lessons and understanding that life is about collaboration and sharing in the good and bad times.

I am grateful to live in this wonderful country, where even after the great confusion of such an immense disaster, help arrived when we needed it the most. The resources were distributed promptly in our city, and cooperation was the order of the day. I also softened my opinion on churches because I witnessed how much good they did every day for years after the storm. And like my dear Mother Mary tells me, they have their job to do. And most of them did an incredible, loving, and compassionate job.

I remember coming back to town for the first time after the disaster and wondering if some of the charities that I had been supporting were going to show up with assistance. One of those charities was Operation Blessing (part of Pat Roberson 700 Club), and even though I don't agree with some of their beliefs, they do run a very good charity, and I love to contribute to a good charity. To my surprise, the first thing I saw on one of our main streets was the big trucks from Operation Blessing. They fed us right away after our long journey back and were there for a long time with hot meals and comforting words. They ran an incredible, efficient operation.

That sure was a nice little lesson for me to see the good in religious organizations and understand that even if we don't agree with their teachings, there is middle ground when love and compassion are the main ingredients.

I also saw the generosity of family, dear friends, and friends of friends who answered the call of compassion during such horrible circumstances. We were blessed to have found hospitality in Tuscaloosa, Alabama. I will forever be grateful to the many people there who comforted us and helped immensely. To all those earth angels, I will be eternally grateful. My prayer is that your generosity serves as the shield that protects you from experiencing such a catastrophe in your own lives. Those and several more lessons I learned, and I am sure, with time, I will discover even more lessons and insights.

We know that natural disasters are a way of life. What are the steps to follow to protect our mental health when disaster strikes, dear Mother?

"Always remember to keep up your spiritual practices and always repeat to yourself and others that every life event is a temporary condition. As you said before, learn to ask for human and divine help and be ready to help others. If you find yourself getting overwhelmed, say a special prayer and gently guide your mind to the task at hand. Keep the company of loved ones and friends and reinforce your faith that a divine plan is unfolding, even if reality seems tragic at the time and life feels overwhelming. Your heavenly family is extremely grateful for the lessons and insights that you were able to understand and pass on to others."

As I was taking a break from writing one day, I read an article in the local newspaper that we are considered the most depressed town in our area. The calls for help from desperate people were divided by zip codes, and the area where Katrina did the most devastation had the highest number of depressed people calling the emergency number. I don't know the statistics before the storm, but I have always suspected that there is a spirit of depression that invaded our city after the storm. I can literally still feel the sadness when I drive past certain areas of my precious city. I believe that Mother Earth is begging for healing and care and that even though most of the material damage was mitigated, there is plenty of work to do on emotional and spiritual healing. This ongoing disease of the soul left by Katrina was followed by the man-made oil spill disaster, and now our healing task has become extremely urgent. I pray daily for the continued healing of my beautiful Slidell.

What can we do, dear Mother, to continue healing Mother Earth and help her mitigate the consequences of these two major disasters?

"It is urgent that people get together in prayer and meditation for the healing of individuals as well as Mother Earth. Adding to the damages caused by both disasters were emotions of anger, fear, and greed. This energy multiplies and keeps on causing more side effects if quick and effective steps are not taken for the healing of all concerned. It is imperative after any disaster to form healing groups to transform damaging thoughts into healing and compassionate thoughts."

Thank you, my Lady. Please help us with this incredible task. We need a major infusion of divine light.

Manifesting Heaven and Hell Like a Pro

I have had periods in my life where I can manifest incredible, wonderful things, but I have also proven to be a specialist in creating some unexplainable messes. I think I finally understand what it takes to know the difference.

I learned of this curse and blessing when I was a young girl. One of my earliest experiences occurred when I was around ten and had become very angry at my mother. I had been sick with the mumps and had been in bed for a few days. A healer had been to my house and had done the usual healing with herbs, advising bed rest. I was ordered by my mother not to leave my bed and not even think about my little excursions down to the river.

I was bored to tears and feeling better, and I missed my walks by the river. I decided to sneak out of bed for some fresh air. The troops from the dictator caught me at my usual spot by the river and brought me back to house arrest. For my little adventure, I was sentenced to a verbal tirade like no other, without permission to voice my excuses. Because I was sick, the spanking would be spared, but I would have preferred the spanking over the long speech.

On my way back to bed, I felt humiliated and extremely angry. While walking to the bedroom, I pronounced with every ounce of my angry, skinny, little body that I would never speak to my mother again.

To my surprise, I felt worse that night, and the fever had returned. My mother decided that she would bring me to the city to see our medical doctor. The doctor treated me and said that I was healing from the mumps, and he assured my mother that I would be fine in a few days. However, the fever had become my best friend, with the added bonus that my voice was totally gone. After another doctor's visit, we were informed that I had developed laryngitis. Again, they treated me and sent me home with the assurance that I would be fine soon. My healing, however, was slow and painful, and my voice was nowhere to be found.

In a couple of weeks, the fever and mumps were history, but my voice had not returned, and no doctors or healers had an answer to the mystery. The school year was approaching, and there was an urgency to get my voice back.

My dear godmother, who was also a teacher at my school, was very worried about me. She came to visit me one day, bearing gifts. She had brought me fruits and all my favorite cookies, and she explained to me that I needed to eat more and that I also needed to get my voice back. She understood me better than my mother, and I admired her greatly. At the end of our visit, she told me that I was healed and that it was all up to me to talk again. She explained to me that I should stand in front of a mirror and start practicing by just saying a few words, starting with something like "Ave Maria." She hugged me and said that she loved me and that she wanted me back to normal.

She had said the magic words—that she loved me, something we never heard at home (we somehow knew that mother loved us, but she would never say the actual words). This caring woman had picked the perfect mantra for me to repeat, and I followed her instructions carefully. I now believe that her visit and her words were definitely an inspiration given directly to her by Mother Mary.

After a few days of looking at myself in the mirror and repeating my mantra, I discovered that sounds were coming out of my throat again. To my amazement and disappointment, I could not recognize my own voice. To this day, I know that my voice never went back to normal, and I lost my ability to sing. But I am grateful to even have a voice and to have had earthly and divine intervention in undoing such a self-harming pronouncement of not speaking to my mother ever again.

On the heavenly side of manifesting, I have also had had some success.

As I was midway into healing my stomach problems, I was driving to my favorite park one day, thinking that I needed a trip to get my joy back to normal and to accelerate my healing. I needed time away to make a plan on healing and conclude the never-ending drama of my on-and-off-again relationship with my boyfriend. I could feel that toxins had invaded my body and my peaceful home. I was thinking of something on a budget and very exciting. I had been out of work for months, and my body still felt weak, but I decided to believe that a miracle would take place.

My mind was telling me that this was impossible; the money supply was low, and I was still on a very strict diet. I told my incredulous mind to shut up and listen, and I decided to make my petition to the universe anyway. I wrote on my petition several places that I wanted to visit—two cities in the USA and cities in Costa Rica and Honduras. I also stated that I wanted to be in a special place meditating on 11/11/11.

(The number 11:11 had been appearing in my life constantly since 2009.)

I stated on my petition that those places would be great, but I was open to suggestions. I checked airplane fares to prove to the universe that I was serious about traveling and to signal my mind to send out traveling frequencies and stop doubting. I said the following statement to myself: *I am expecting a beautiful and healing trip, and it will be provided by the loving energy of the universe.*

I meditated and visualized my trip and kept it a secret infused with love and faith. I placed my petition on my altar and let it go.

In a span of approximately two weeks, little pieces of the puzzle began arriving. I am fortunate to know and socialize with people of many nationalities. One day, a friend who lives in my town, but who is originally from Spain, called me with an unusual request. She told me that a friend of hers was visiting from the Canary Islands, Spain, and she could use some help with transportation and translating. She wanted to know if I could offer some help and meet her at her house. I told her that I was always ready to welcome new people into my life and would love to be of assistance.

My new friend and I liked each other the minute we met and found out that we had many things in common. I took her around town, and one day as we were having lunch, she offered me her house if I ever wanted to visit Spain again. I said, "I hope you mean it because I love to travel." I also mentioned that I thought that traveling to Europe was probably a little too much for my budget now, but I would take her up on her offer in the future. However, in the back of my mind, I wondered if this was already a first sign from the universe.

When I brought her back to our mutual friend's house, as we were visiting and enjoying a cup of tea, we talked about the invitation she had extended to me. Friend number one told me, "I will be going to Spain in a couple of months, and you can come along so you do not have to travel by yourself."

I said, "Let me go home and run some numbers, but it would take a miracle for a trip in a couple of months." My angels were telling me to pay attention, but my mind was in total doubt that such a trip could be possible.

A couple of days later, friend number one called to ask me if I had given any more thought to the trip. She advised me that I should consider the offer because I would not have to pay for hotel rooms and that my new friend owned a beautiful and comfortable penthouse with close access to everything in the city.

This was beginning to get interesting. Did I hear *penthouse in an out-of-this-world downtown*? And she added a special detail: if I was really interested, she could get a discounted ticket through another friend of hers. I told my angels, "Okay, I am paying attention now. Is this the trip that I prayed for?" My whole being was getting excited. I would have to coordinate a few things and get ready, but I could manage. I was making mental notes: my camera broke, my clothes didn't fit anymore because I had lost a lot of weight, and I had not been to the shopping mall in months. I told her I would pray about it and get back with her.

I stayed up late that night, praying and meditating, and the next morning, I woke up overjoyed with the email of my mind telling me, "Go for it. We did better than you thought." This trip had been divinely arranged. I responded with a big thank you, and from that moment on, I knew that everything would fall into place.

Indeed, everything fell into place. A friend sent me a cash gift to buy a new camera, and little gifts of unexpected cash and forgotten refunds started arriving in an incredible, steady flow. People who owed me money paid back, and others who didn't even know that I was planning a trip were very generous to me.

The angels even arranged for a free reading worth several hundred dollars from a fantastic angel named Dee Wallace. I had made an appointment with her office, but somehow the timing was not right, and I canceled. My cancelation got lost in angelic cyberspace, and I received her call anyway. She is such a beautiful being and said, "Since we are already talking, do you want a free reading?" I started by complaining about my list of diseases and lack of money. When she heard that in a few days I was flying to Spain, she immediately said, "My dear, you are thriving." Magical words, my dear lady. Your sweet voice and insights were the icing on my cake. Thank you so much for having crossed my path at such a delicate time in my life. I love you forever and send you love and hugs always.

Every detail for my beautiful trip was coordinated with precision by heavenly and earth angels. We started by staying in Madrid for a couple of nights with my friend's friends. I was hosted and treated like royalty by people I was meeting for the first time. The hospitality that I experienced was a tremendous blessing at that time in my life.

After our stay in Madrid, we flew to Santa Cruz de Tenerife, where I spent three incredible weeks hosted by the most generous earth angel. I met incredible people who showered me with attention and the most delicious food and wine. I went to wonderful parties and luncheons, and my dear stomach never complained. I was in total gratitude, and my body felt energized and healthy. This was definitely the answer to my prayers.

The cities I visited in the Canary Islands were without a doubt some of the most beautiful places on this earth. I was privileged to visit El Teide, which is a gorgeous and majestic volcano, with an energy flow that is one of the strongest and purest I have ever experienced in my life. A few hours spent on this wonder of the world was enough to do the job that no medicine had done for me. The healing effects were going to stay with me for the rest of my life.

I spent 11/11/11 meditating at 11:00 a.m. on the rooftop of my friend's penthouse, overlooking the city and its beautiful surroundings. As I was contemplating the city on this special day, I was overwhelmed with gratitude for the manifestation of such a marvelous trip, done with very little money. I made a promise to myself and my heavenly family that I would finish putting my story in writing to inspire others to trust in their inner guidance and the generosity of the universe and humanity. Just as there are people who would steal your salvaged belongings during a horrible catastrophe, there are also people who will lift you up, help you touch heaven, and show you the other side of human nature.

I have come to realize that the law of attraction does work, and one of the main keys to getting your desires fulfilled is asking clearly and joyfully, meditating and visualizing the best outcome, and then letting the universe work on your petition at its own timing and design. I realize that there are other approaches, and I have tried many others, but I have had more success by using the one described above. This approach has worked for me even before I was conscious of manifesting my desires, as happened when I moved to the United States.

When I moved to the United States, I went to school immediately. After classes, I enjoyed window-shopping in beautiful downtown New Orleans. I used to marvel at the beautiful city and felt grateful for the opportunity to go to school in such cosmopolitan surroundings. One day as I was coming back from school and admiring the well-dressed women coming out of the buildings, I looked up at one of the tallest buildings by the river front. Without thinking, I made the following pronouncement: "One day, I will work in that beautiful building."

Years passed, and when I was ready to start working, I registered with an employment agency. They sent me to several interviews that included an international bank in the building mentioned before. To my amazement, as I entered the building, I remembered my affirmation, and I knew instantly that this would be the place for my first working opportunity.

The interview went great, and to my further amazement, one of the women interviewing me was a good friend of the owner of the company I had worked for back in my country. I had never met this lady, but I had heard my old boss mention her in conversation, and she had also heard about me. When she saw my work history, she was extremely surprised at how small the world seems to be sometimes. That reference was enough to seal the deal.

On my ride home on public transportation, I was trying to figure that out and comprehend the workings of the universe. When I started interviewing, I was worried that my main work reference in this country was of a nanny and not office work. Which forces were at work that resulted in my employment from back home being the main key to obtaining this exciting new job? And what were the chances of that synchronicity happening in a lifetime? As I was entering my apartment, the telephone rang, and I rushed to answer, knowing that an offer was waiting for me at the other end of the line. The human resources manager of the bank was on the telephone, offering me the job with a better salary than I had imagined.

Lesson learned. While I was employed back home, I knew that the job had no future potential, but I felt grateful to be working since my country was always in an employment crisis, so I performed my work with love and efficiency. I have to thank my dear dictator mother for teaching me gratitude and work ethic. The references that my former boss provided for me where impeccable, and she urged her friend to hire me immediately.

This is one of my most memorable manifesting experiences. In the instant that I made my pronouncement of future employment, I was in complete joy and gratitude. I also remember having a type of innocence, like a child expecting good things. That innocence was also sprinkled with trust and letting go. I don't remember ever dwelling on the fact that I was going to work there or how it was going to happen. I was like a child writing a letter to Santa, knowing that Santa would deliver.

When I have let myself descend into worry and confusion, I have made incredible messes and detrimental decisions. The more I pay attention to the manifesting laws of the universe, the more I have learned to use my words wisely and to be vigilant with my thoughts. Let's start manifesting the right way.

MY SOULMATE FROM HELL

The signs that I was about to embark on the mother of all adventures were presented to me even before I met him, but after my separation, I was out to prove to myself and the world that I was still a beautiful and attractive woman. I was totally naïve and out of date with dating tactics. My dating career had ended in my early twenties, and I had no idea of the skills possessed by a man determined to get what he wanted.

My first warning came from a friend who was divorced. She gave me the advice to be careful and to take my time before dating again. But it was hopeless. I had just met my soulmate, and I was convinced that he was a gift from Venus herself. He looked like Antonio Banderas, danced like John Travolta, could bite his lip like Bill Clinton, and sang in my ear like Julio Iglesias. What was a girl to do when her self-esteem had packed its bags and departed the same day her husband moved out?

My savior was younger than me, and he spoke of hope and change way before President Obama made those words famous. My soulmate and greatest teacher came to me with all these attributes but also with a challenging addiction to alcohol and childhood traumas.

My poor guides were busy trying to get my attention, and about a week before I met him, I had the strangest dream. My dear godfather passed away from complications of alcoholism. In my dream, I was visiting with my godfather, and I could see hundreds of others who had died from addictions, including one of my brothers. They were all lying on a cold floor in a grayish-looking room, and they invited me to come join them. I reluctantly accepted the invitation, but as soon as I joined them, a row of heavy chains connected me to all of them. I tried to move but felt incapable of doing so. I felt paralyzed and completely attached to them. I woke up scared to death but decided to ignore the dream as a stupid nightmare due to all the stress that I had been experiencing lately. I should have known by then that I get powerful guidance in my dreams, but I dismissed it.

A few weeks after I met him, I was speaking to a lady who knew him, and she told me, "He is a good worker and a very generous man, but he has a powerful addiction." My heart skipped a beat as I remembered the dream. Was that dream a warning from my beloved godfather? *Oh, but his promises are of making changes just for me. He only drinks because he is lonely, and he assures me that with my love, the change is just around the corner.* Little did I know that it was an unreachable corner that kept moving constantly. Like a true rescue trooper, I set out on the adventure of several lifetimes, to say the least.

To prove his undying love for me, he suggested that he would move from his state to mine, and I was, of course, overjoyed at this incredible show of undeserved love and attention. Nobody had ever shown so much love and sacrifice for me. The truth was that he was in debt up to his drunken eyeballs, and he had thugs looking for him for past betting debts. Of course, he informed me that this had happened at a time when he did not have the love of such a special woman. Together, we were going to slay his addiction forever. I believed in the fairy tale, mounted my unicorn, and invited all the addiction spirits into my life.

After a brief long-distance romance, he moved to my state, and we embarked on a life of incredible highs and lows. Anybody who has lived with an alcoholic knows well what I am talking about.

I admit that the good times were a needed escape from my complicated life at the time. We both enjoyed dancing and cooking, and his sense of humor could keep me entertained for hours. But as the years went by, the good times were less often, and his habit was becoming that horrible chain of my earlier dream. Big arguments replaced the good times, and his financial mistakes were numerous. I felt totally paralyzed in making a decision to free myself from the chains.

After Hurricane Katrina, his drinking increased at an incredible pace, and I decided to ask my guides to help me end my mysterious attachment to this man. Like clockwork, my angels worked things with incredible precision, and he was out of my apartment within two weeks of my prayer. Round one. I was weak and dizzy but still standing.

As I said before, I put my life back together after Katrina and was granted some incredible gifts of good timing by the universe. I found a house in a part of town that had never flooded before; however, I could not put this man out of my mind. He invaded my dream time and my daily thought life. And of course, he was part of my family by then, and he was included in family festivities. One of my sons has a daughter, and he wanted to be a part of his step-granddaughter's life.

He never missed an opportunity to make more promises and to assure me that he was sober and had definitely learned his lesson. I was in a good place financially and emotionally, but against all my instincts, I went for round two. I was ready for more punishment; after all, I had had a nice, long break. I agreed to start seeing him as friends on a wait-and-see basis. After a few weeks of friendship and great times, he seemed perfectly fine, and I invited him to dinner at my house and to spend the night in the spare bedroom.

My angels stared working overtime again. That very same night, I had a dream that I was working in a new office, and on my first day of employment, someone dumped a body tightly wrapped in a blanket in the middle of the office.

Several people were working there, but they were avoiding looking in that direction, and I decided to just leave and quit. I went downstairs to leave, but I encountered the biggest maze I had ever seen. There was no way out. Everywhere I turned, there were big obstacles and locked gates. It was a terrifying experience, and I woke up scared and angry. My guides gently helped me to calm down and encouraged me to write the dream in my journal.

I prayed and went back to sleep. To make sure I got the message, the dream appeared again. I woke up and read my notes, and the details were the same. I knew that getting together with this man could mean endless U-turns and ups and downs again, and my guides were desperate to let me know.

Against all my inner alarms, I ignored the warning and chose to believe his story that he was sober. After a few weeks of being together, the drinking started again, but this time, I was smarter; we would not combine households.

After several months of broken promises, I put an end to the fairy tale. For a while, I was happy, making new friends. I had blocked his number and only heard of him through friends.

I only remembered him occasionally, but the holidays were coming, and the rescuer in me was whispering, "Help the poor, peace on earth, and love to all." I made that dreaded phone call to see how he was doing, and he informed me that he was a new man and ready to make things up to me.

He was again talking of change and hope, and now had added "Yes we can."

I agreed to meet him for lunch. We went to a beautiful restaurant with a big picture window that overlooked the small downtown of the city where he had moved a few years before. As soon as I took my first bite, I looked out the beautiful window, and the scene outside left me speechless. It was a funeral procession. I almost choked on my food, because I knew that my angels had figured out that I was totally stupid, pretending to be smart, and they would now send me the signals in my awake hours, because I seemed to be ignoring the dreams.

I dismissed the sign as just a coincidence and my active imagination. Besides, his talk of change was totally mesmerizing. I chose to believe him, and round three proved to be more devastating than the previous rounds. His habit was ready to deliver the knockout punch.

We were planning our future together again. However, the only change seemed to be his ability to hide his drinking better. This time, he talked me into moving with me again. After all, if I loved him, I should share my blessings with him, and by being close to me, he could work on his recovery with more power and enthusiasm.

Moving day came, and the minute I arrived at his house to help him pack, I was hit with a stabbing stomach pain, and I felt nauseated and sick. My poor body was desperate and trying to make me react. But like the good rescuer that I am, risking my health was a small price to pay for true love. After all, this man assured me that his love was even greater now after all these years.

In addition to dealing with his addiction, I also had an incredibly demanding job, and my body was feeling the stress from several fronts. In the span of a few months, I was given diagnoses for seven different ailments, all related to my stomach power center.

I had an hour drive to see my doctors at the hospital, and my angels were still busy sending signals. The drive was through a country highway, and to my surprise, every time I was going for an appointment, there was a funeral procession in progress. This was totally creepy, and by now, I was questioning my angels' tactics. What were the chances that in such desolate, little towns, there was a funeral scheduled every time I had an appointment? But I should have known better. Divine timing is not easy to comprehend for the human mind, and my angels had figured out that the signals were now to be sent in broad daylight.

I spoke to my angels loudly and clearly and told them, "Okay, I get the message. I will untangle this situation as soon as possible." By then, the doctors had taken a stomach biopsy because they were suspecting stomach cancer. I made a deal with my heavenly family, asking them to help me with the results of the biopsy, and I, in turn, would heal the relationship once and for all. In that instant, I felt the power of my intention possessing every cell of my body and granting me a determination to heal all this drama that was affecting my complete being.

The biopsy turned out to be negative, and I knew that for my own salvation, I had to follow through with my promise. I was relieved at the results and prayed with gratitude and assured Mother Mary that I was totally firm in my resolve to break away from my repeating patterns with my soulmate. I told her that she could send my spooky angels on a deserved vacation. I continued with my treatments, and to my delight, I saw no more funeral processions.

I explained to him that this was our final round and that this time I was armed with resolve and divine courage. He would have to make a decision to work with me in figuring out our karma, or it was finally over. His controlling tactics came out in force, even implying that it was my fault that he drank because I nagged him too much about it. This was the icing on the cake for my resolve. I was furious and gifted him with a few flying objects. I told him that I was not the alcoholic—I was an enabler and a rescuer—but that I was giving up those titles, and from now on, my efforts were going to be devoted to my own good and enlightenment.

I decided to enlist Archangel Michael for this immense task to help us heal or go on with our lives, separate or together. At this point, I had accepted any outcome. We talked about love being eternal and that it would be with us always, whether we were together or apart.

I spent hours meditating and listening to divine guidance to figure out our bonds of deep love but also of extreme pain. One early morning as I was meditating, Archangel Michael asked me the following question: "Who was by your side to hold you and console you when you were having those nightmares related to your trauma of sexual abuse?" I was totally speechless. My soulmate, of course, and he had showed true love and compassion during that difficult period of my life. Archangel Michael also explained to me that hiding behind that alcoholic man was true light and love.

On another communication with Archangel Michael, he totally

surprised me again with the following question: "What kind of soulmate are you to him?" He had asked the questions that would unlock all the answers to our past and present karma. Of course, if I put myself in his shoes, I could see that it required a great effort on his part to help me deal with my emotional baggage. I could switch from an angel to a lunatic in an instant, with no help from any stimulants.

After deep meditations and prayer, a portal was opened, and the answers began arriving. The point for us being together was that we had to conclude unfinished business from a recent past life. When we planned our next lives, we had an agreement that we would be each other's strongest teacher. We had agreed that the love would be immense to help protect each other from the big task ahead of us. That love was essential to my emotional healing when the draining nightmares related to my childhood trauma terrorized me.

One of the first clues to our past life together came in a dream. I could see our past life with total clarity—the cast of characters, the country where that life had taken place, the scenery, the circumstances, the people we had loved, and the people we had hurt. I saw every detail of our wrongdoings and our selfish acts. Some of the people in that life whom we had hurt were causing us difficulties in this life. I experienced an incredible awakening within that dream.

After I woke up, I remembered how we had met this time around. His first words to me were "I have seen you in my dreams." I laughed and said, "Great pickup line," but in reality, the minute we met, he felt totally comfortable with me. I was reluctant to get to know him, but I also felt comfortable with him, and somehow we both knew that we had ties to a mysterious past. We ended up talking and dancing all night.

My youngest son was also involved in that past life, and when they met in this present life, it was instant rapport and recognition of previous ties. This was totally puzzling to me at the time, because my son was jealous and very protective of me, but he let his guard down immediately and welcomed him into our lives.

The person that we had double-crossed in that past life was the person who introduced us in this life. She insisted that I needed to go out and meet this friend of her friend who was in town on vacation and was a great dancer. I was totally exhausted that day, and a good night's sleep sounded heavenly. I made up many excuses, but she and another friend showed up at my house anyway. They kept insisting that a night of dancing was the right prescription and that I needed to meet new people.

With subsequent dreams and visions, the total picture came into my mind. Together we had caused plenty of pain in that past life. We had acted with no compassion and had destroyed the security of others; therefore, we had agreed to meet again in this life and work on compassion, communication, protection, security, and forgiveness.

My biggest surprise with all these revelations was that my father had agreed to be my father to help me prepare for the hard road ahead. I was totally shocked by this piece of information. I had blamed this man for being weak and detached, but in reality, he had accepted an awful supporting role to be my first teacher in the addiction classroom.

I was given the privilege to see in one of the visions that my father is actually an extremely evolved soul and that we had had several lifetimes together. It was explained to me that what I had perceived as weakness was actually to teach me strength, and what I had perceived as detachment was to teach me nonattachment and self-reliance. This beautiful vision was an incredible, loving gesture from my guides, and I was filled with infinite love and gratitude for my deceased father who had carried that heavy cross of alcoholism during this lifetime.

As a child, I had perceived glimpses of his advanced soul, and I could read his love for me when he was sober. He was a man of few words, and we could spend hours in silence just enjoying each other's company. I would watch him work in his shop for hours. He was a genius at repairing any type of electrical equipment. He was a musician and a self-taught electrician and mechanic whose services where in high demand, but he would withdraw from the public for months at a time. My dad made his transition years ago, but a side effect from all this work has been that I have made peace with my dad, and I could sense his love for me even more after this revelation.

In another vision after deep meditation and fasting, I was given the privilege of seeing more of the planning steps to this present lifetime. It is a very delicate undertaking of calculations and possibilities. I was totally fascinated by what appeared to be a space of light, sounds, and numbers. The equipment is beyond description, and our computers here would seem like toys in comparison. There appeared to be millions of calculations going on at the same time for the new life, but somehow every entry was treated as extremely special and worthy of the most reverence and love.

This out-of-this-world equipment was with very advanced beings of the light. They knew that every calculation was of extreme importance for a new life's mission. The sophisticated equipment was guided by wisdom only—no buttons to push, just an intelligent observation tower with minor adjustments being made by an all-knowing system.

It appeared to me that even the name of the new traveler was chosen in a sense. I remember very clearly that they referred to us as travelers. A specific name was not picked but instead sounds and numbers that could fit several names to choose from, which would be essential for the new traveler. Astrological calculations were also added in this light space. It was a strange and fascinating mixture of details.

This reminded me of a shaman who would walk for miles to find the specific herb needed for a healing. No effort was spared for the success of the mission.

Another surprise was that one of the calculations for our next life was that we could not have a child together due to having misused this privilege in our previous life. Apparently, we were not very good parents in that lifetime. This stipulation was essential to undoing a tremendous amount of karma. To mitigate this stipulation, we would have other opportunities together to show our love to children. We were in the knowing that this was for our growth and highest good. We felt totally loved by our guides, and our reaction was a complete feeling of gratitude. (When we met in this lifetime, I had already had a tubal ligation, and he had been told by doctors that he was not able to have children.)

During this vision, I asked my guides if every detail of a life is previously determined. I was reminded that we are born with all the knowledge of creation encoded in our DNA. We are also equipped with the potential of discovering the information. What makes the adventure so enticing is knowing that in order to decode this information, we have to be great detectives and work our way out from darkness to light again. The wisdom is in us at all times, but it gets clouded by the material realm. They advised me that one day we will be able to decode this information in our early stages of life, and suffering will be on its way out. Love will replace fear, and we will be able to pronounce that the kingdom of heaven has arrived on earth.

During this period, I also understood that we do not arrive on earth to be victims or perpetrators; we come with the outlined lessons on compassion, forgiveness, peace, and so on. As we travel our road, our vision can become cloudy, and without a spiritual practice, we can become totally lost. I also understood that when we misuse our opportunities, eventually we come back with a more difficult curriculum. Please be assured that this is not seen as punishment by the returning soul; it is understood that it is the law of the universe to purify the planet and magnify love. Occasionally, a more evolved soul will volunteer to be part of our next experience in order to assist with the mission.

I also understood that we have a choice of aborting the mission when it has become extremely painful. My angels were giving me the chance to do just that when they were giving me all those dreams and signals. I had the choice to run or prepare myself and fasten my seat belt. In some part of our being, we still have the memory of the plan and a deep commitment to fulfill it. We use the wrong tools for the project when we try to accomplish our mission without divine guidance.

I had unconsciously become his enabler and rescuer in an effort to master my lesson on compassion, but now my fits of anger were doing nothing to teach him compassion or communication. His overspending on presents to make up for his drinking was doing absolutely nothing to teach me protection and security.

Archangel Michael also made me realized that there is absolutely no heavenly punishment for walking away from a situation or person that has become dangerous and too much of a burden for us to face. The choice is always ours to protect ourselves and ask for divine and earthly assistance. During this healing period, my boyfriend had to move to another state for work reasons, and I was underemployed at the time. He had the ability to manifest employment quickly, and within a few weeks, he was helping me financially. One day as I was talking to Archangel Michael, I asked him, "Do you think this is my chance to make a clean break from him?"

He gave me the funniest face and said, "Why now when he is far away and sending you money?"

I went into uncontrolled laughter and said, "Yes, that would be me. I run when things are getting better and stay for punishment when things are bad." Archangel Michael has a big sense of humor.

After all this information was given to me, I felt totally energized and grateful for the understanding that it is a grand plan and that when we conclude the lessons, we reach higher states of wisdom and choice.

One day, as I was driving to the hospital for some lab work, I saw many cars and what appeared to be a funeral procession. I yelled at the top of my lungs, "Not again! I am cured! No more creepy signals!" But as I got closer to a little country church, I realized that it was a wedding taking place, and I couldn't contain my joy and laughter at the sense of humor of my angels. This was my time for renewal and the beginning of the next chapter of my seriously crazy life. Heaven has perfect timing, and I was working on the wedding feast chapter of this book when I saw the little country wedding.

I am a work in progress. My addiction to punishment was cured once I realized that I was trying to fulfill my life lessons using the wrong tools and outdated technology. My angels sure worked overtime trying to save me from myself, and they used every tactic to get my attention. I realized that they used the death symbolism to make me understand that I needed to look at my past life's connections. They also wanted to emphasize that addictions are deadly, whether you are addicted to alcohol, drugs, punishment, or another human being. I hated to admit that I had some kind of addiction, because I always boasted that I had never had any addictions in my life—except chocolate, of course. I was perishing for lack of knowledge, like the Bible says. My body protested from all the stress, and my emotional being was in despair for not knowing how to solve our problems without compromising our love.

I have no need to revisit this lesson again in this life or a future one. I love and congratulate myself for having had the guts to work this out, and I tell myself so every day. My angelic internet is getting better, and I rejoice in the fact that I have a broader view of our earth assignments and the life after.

He admits that he was comfortable in my care and did not see the urgency to seek help. Our love for each other is still intact, but it has been transformed into a love between good friends. I have helped him with my angelic teachings, but I understand that he has more work to do on his additional contracts and the rest of his sacred mission. He had a difficult childhood and has more work on forgiveness and healing ahead of him. It is all up to him to get off the cross and work on his own resurrection.

We have also come to the understanding that our past-life karma has been resolved, and we have undone all those ties from previous life encounters. The death symbolism that my guides were frantically using was signaling to search beyond this present life. After I meditated on undoing any past-life contracts, I felt that the final phase of the healing process had taken place for me, and I hoped for him also.

The biggest compliment that he has given me is that he is working on discovering his inner light and that he is grateful to me for teaching him the tools for this search. He had many problems with his mother, and he has found great joy in developing a relationship with Mother Mary. He now understands her great love and compassion. On one of my angry outbursts with Mother Mary, I asked her if she hated him as much as I did. Her response totally floored me. She said, "I love him just as I love you." Big wake-up call for me. I thought all that time that I deserved more love from her. She explained to me that every human being is worthy of her unconditional love. I got off my unicorn that day and told her, "He is all yours. My days of rescuer and enabler are over, and our karma has left the building."

I have also learned many lessons from him and will always remember that his love and care for those around him are unconditionally given.

His love for our granddaughter is totally unconditional. She is the only person who can make him forget his addiction. The times spent playing with her were the most peaceful times I had been able to recognize in him; he would turn into another four-year-old, with no anger or painful memories. For this true love, I am totally grateful. We can laugh now and help each other as true friends without any codependency. He is thrilled that I am telling his story in the hope of making a difference in others struggling with recurring patterns beyond our normal human understanding. He also agrees with the title of his chapter, and we had some good laughs while choosing it.

After long talks and devising a system to salvage our friendship, I am happy to admit that we have reached the point of infinite love and compassion for each other, but what a ride we had to get to this point. We have gone our separate ways, and I pray daily that he keeps his resolve to finally undo his addiction, but if he chooses to resume that habit, it is not my job to save him. Our conflicts have been resolved, but as I said, he still has other issues to untangle. It is his own decision. I will respect that decision. I am at peace knowing that I did my best to share with him the freedom tools that I have been given by my guides. I am celebrating my freedom from this karma issue and planning a life of more wonder and joy. Namaste!

THE WEDDING FEAST

I am so grateful and excited for your help with the mystery of the first miracle. My first question is the meaning of his saying, "Unless you are born again, you cannot enter the kingdom of heaven." Do we need to get baptized as an adult to reach this kingdom?

"The baptism is a symbolism that indicates that you are ready to claim your divinity because in water resides the memories of everything that you are. Water remembers that you are a divine being and reminds you to claim your heavenly citizenship.

"Both birth and rebirth have fluidity as symbols. When a new child is ready to make its appearance on earth, the breaking of the water as known in plain language puts the world on notice that the birth is imminent.

"When you decide to let spirit be your guide, by using the power of water, you put heaven on notice that you are ready to remember the real you and that you are eager to accomplish your sacred mission. Just as new babies are welcome and assisted by a team of experts and relatives, human beings claiming their divinity will be guided and assisted as well by a team of beings in the spiritual realm.

"When you make the commitment to claim your divinity, you are claiming your right to enjoy a human experience on earth, as well as accepting the truth that you are and always will be an eternal spirit."

Does it make any difference when and where baptism takes place?

"The ritual will not make any difference if you are still attached to your old beliefs. Transformation takes place when you are ready to discover your true origins and live your life as a guest of earth but a citizen of heaven. The transformation will be felt whether you are doing the dishes or walking on the shores of a beautiful beach."

Is a second baptism necessary if a person has been baptized as an infant?

"The rituals of earth are beneficial for your journey. We are honored when you dedicate time to such beautiful ceremonies at any stage of life. However, the rituals of heaven are subtle and take place in your own internal and personal space; therefore, anytime and anywhere that you make the commitment to claim your divine heritage, it is accepted and celebrated joyfully in the heavenly realms."

I remember the beautiful rituals in my village when a baby was born. The baby was bathed by loving grandmothers, aunts, and female neighbors and gently massaged with aromatic oils and herbs. The baby was then dressed in handmade clothes and blankets and blessed by the women present. Could this be considered a baptism?

"That is a beautiful example of ancestral blessings and welcoming the new baby into a loving community. Such rituals are considered a powerful baptism."

I know many adults who have been baptized but leave the church even sadder when they are reminded that they are pitiful sinners not worthy of God's grace and that they will burn in hell for their transgressions. I left several churches for this same reason.

"My dear, you figured out the real secret later on, and now you have the necessary tools for self-transformation."

Yes, I do. It took years of meditation and observation—and your help, of course. I am still learning, but let me share my insights, and let me know if I have grasped the main teachings.

I have always been fascinated by the miracles that Jesus performed, and the first known miracle of changing the water into wine kept reminding me that there was a great mystery in that miracle that had to do with our self-transformation. The story tells me that he enjoyed a good party and that he was an important guest at the wedding in Cana. This, of course, is not in agreement with some of the Christian teachings of suffering and sin. I never understood why dancing and enjoying a good time could be considered a sin.

I understood some parts of the wedding feast in our conversations when I was a young girl. Like the fact that he used this miracle to instill faith in his disciples. And the fact that you were the one who asked him made me believe in your intercessory gift, not just at the wedding feast but in our everyday life.

However, I knew that there was something deeper in the story, having to do with personal transformation. Slowly I began to realize that being born again is gently training our mind and soul into being guided by spirit.

In other words, turning water into wine. When we awaken to spirit, we become capable of creating the kingdom of heaven here on earth. We can have the best of both worlds. When we are in the kingdom, we are happy and abundant, and at the wedding feast, there was great joy after the better wine was manifested.

The party was good, but it must have gotten great after the good wine was presented. I interpret this as a reflection of our lives. Before transformation, we might be managing life, but after transformation, we are in a better position to achieve greater states of joy and well-being and to truly enjoy our successes in life.

When we are new creatures, we have the best of both worlds, because spirit guides us through the material realm. When we turn on the light within, we are born again, and we enjoy heaven on earth. We need both aspects to be grounded on the material plane, but we need to be guided by spirit in order to avoid despair when life hits us with unexpected challenges.

What do you think, my dear Lady? Will I climb another step on my ascension ladder today?

"I am certainly impressed, my dear child. Please stay inspired and keep up your spiritual practice."

What would be the best percentage of matter and spirit?

"I know that you have figured out that mystery too."

After my incredible visit to the Hall of Light, I know numbers are very important in creation. The portion of water in the human body varies, but it is usually calculated around 70 percent. If we live our lives knowing that we are spiritual beings using the water analogy, we are in ascension city. Babies have more than that; no wonder they can easily see the other side.

I was also excited to make the comparison with our chakras or energy centers. At this time in our ascension process, we are working with seven main chakras. Spirit flows from our crown chakra down to the other six to purify and transform our bodies. Once this transformation takes place, we are definitely first class, just like the wine at the wedding feast.

In other words, the six stone jars that were filled with water at the wedding feast represent our chakras or energy centers. These six energy centers run from our lower-body root chakra to our upper-body third eye chakra. Water represents the divine substance that flows from the energy center at the top of our head, called the crown chakra. Once they are illuminated, it becomes easier to move our energy from the lower chakras to the upper chakras, merge with the divine, and attain oneness. We are born again of the water, which represents spirit, and we enter the kingdom of heaven on earth. Before transformation, we are just stone pots, useful but without fluidity.

So what do you think? Have I understood the main point?

"You are on your way, my child, but let me make one observation. Please don't get too preoccupied with exact percentages. Each individual is working on his or her personal ascension. Even a slight shift is transforming and beneficial to the individual and to the entire planet. The more you feed from spirit, the more you will delight in the results, and your progress becomes steady and enjoyable. Only totally dedicated yogis, monks, and devoted people of certain religions operate in the higher percentage of spirit. If every human being on earth shifted slightly to more spirit, the illumination and transformation would end world conflicts immediately. I hope that I am making myself clear. It is a steady and daily advance that will accomplish great levels of improvement and joy."

Yes. I think I understand. The key is in the daily commitment to be in the flow of the lovely marriage of heaven and earth. Do you have any more advice to make the road to enlightenment easier and more enjoyable?

"My advice is to keep studying the great mysteries. Be diligent with your spiritual practices and enjoy every minute of the beautiful material plane."

Thank you, my beautiful Lady. I am definitely excited about the road I have taken.

As she advised, I kept on studying this great mystery and set out to unravel more secrets. The story starts in John 2:1–12, which says that after three days, there was a marriage in Cana of Galilee.

I was well advanced in unraveling the story and did not pay much attention to the fact that the story starts by saying, "After three days, there was a wedding in Cana." One day as I was writing, a question was placed in what I call my email of the mind. "What do you think those three days signify?" I was somewhat annoyed, because I knew it would take me many days of meditation to figure that out. But the email also said, "Ask and you shall receive." I surrendered totally to spirit and my guides and said the following statement: *I am open to receiving all the information and insights pertaining to this great mystery because I know that this information is essential for enlightenment.*

I sent them the message, knowing that they would respond accordingly.

One morning as I was drinking a cup of tea, the email of my mind was turned on, and I got the information needed. The email read, "Remember that the scriptures were encoded with great mysteries and secrecy, and this is the era of revelation."

My first reaction was "I hope you don't mean that I have to read the book of Revelation." I was thinking they wanted me to read the book in the Bible that has terrified many people for centuries.

The angels laughed with me and informed me that reading that book would be my next assignment. And then they gave me the piece of information I needed. "Please do not think in terms of days." This is the fascinating part of working with your spiritual guides. They will give you part of the answer, and then they will make you work for the rest. They use this method to help us sharpen our intuition. I set out to figure it out during my morning walk. I started with another question: could three days mean weeks, months, or years? By now, I knew their tricks—they love for me to ask questions. This is a spiritual rule: if you ask the question, they will answer. Ask and you shall receive.

I was enjoying my walk, admiring nature, and thinking about calling one of my sons (who would be turning thirty in a few weeks) to plan a lunch date. Suddenly, bells went off in my mind. *It is three decades they are talking about, not three days.* Jesus started his ministry at thirty years of age. No wonder the wedding miracle was his first major miracle. He himself had just been baptized and claimed his divinity. I was so excited about making the connection. I am not that slow after all!

Most humans are just getting into maturity at around that age, meaning that thirty is the perfect time to make our commitment to the marriage of heaven and earth. It is most definitely a good age for human marriage too.

The story of the wedding feast goes on saying that the Mother of Jesus was there. This makes me believe that she had arrived earlier to assist the family with the wedding preparations. This puts a big smile on my face. I can hear the whispers of my paternal grandmother ("If there was no Mary, there would be no Jesus"). If she was chosen to be the mother of our great master, she is a special master herself. She is meant to play an important part in our own marriage of heaven and earth.

Later on, Jesus and his entourage arrived, just when the wine was running out. If we invite him to our own wedding feast, he will be happy to show us how to awaken to spirit and produce the good wine. His mother felt comfortable asking him for a favor on behalf of others. She was the link between Jesus and the servants. She is still our link between earth and the higher dimensions.

The servants could not go straight to Jesus because he was greeting people and enjoying the festivities with the important guest at the feast. There was no possibility for the servants to reach this inner circle. Without enlightenment, humans cannot reach the high levels of consciousness necessary to unite with the light, where there is plenty of the good wine.

The women of the gathering were, as usual, making sure that things were running smoothly; therefore, his mother was more accessible. She could mingle with the women and the servants and be respected and welcomed in the VIP section, because she was an important guest herself. She has a special dispensation to come to our spiritual level and bring our troubles to the higher heavenly realms, where solutions abound.

She was informed of the problem and went immediately to him, stating, "We need your help; there is no wine." He addressed her as Woman and explained to her that the timing for miracles had not yet arrived. His answer has always been intriguing to me. I have heard people and many scholars who have misinterpreted his answer as Jesus being annoyed or disrespectful to his mother.

Actually, Mother Mary informs me that the word *Woman* coming out of his lips was a great honor that he conferred to those women close to him. He valued and admired the role of women in his ministry and his life. This was a tender moment between mother and son, and he was pleased to accept his mother's petition. She knew that he was ready, and she was confident that he could salvage the situation.

He had not expected to put his divine power to work yet, but he was absolutely delighted to grant his mother this favor on behalf of others. As was then, so it is now. He always attends her petitions on our behalf.

She then commanded the servants, telling them, "Do as he says." She has command of a multitude of angels in both realities.

Jesus ordered the servants to fill the six water pots with water. The master used his power after receiving her petition. The wine was manifested, and Jesus advised the servants to present the results to the governor of the feast. The servants followed orders and presented the new wine to the governor of the feast, who raved about the excellent product.

Who is the governor of the feast? The governor of the feast is the Creator, of course, who is proud of every one of us and raves when we access his wisdom. There is great joy in heaven when we cooperate with one another. Whoever saw the problem quietly enlisted her help, and she immediately went for his assistance. When we ask for her assistance, she is quick to act on our behalf.

There was one thing that puzzled me immensely though. During meditation, I was given the insight that the governor or ruler of the feast was the Creator himself. But then the story says that when he tasted the wine, he did not know where it came from, but the servants did. If he is all-knowing, what is really the hidden mystery here?

It took several days of pondering and asking my guides for answers to finally arrive at this very important answer. I decided to take a break from writing and let them guide me, to wait for divine timing. I went to bed one night remembering a conversation I had with Mother Mary when she had said, "We all rejoice when you reach enlightenment, no matter which road has been taken."

To my surprise, as I was waking up the next morning, the visions started to flood my mind. I saw the people arriving at the wedding feast. And believe me, this was a first-class wedding. A modern-day celebrity wedding would pale in comparison.

There were great caravans of wealthy people. I saw beautiful carriages and animals carrying great treasures and personal belongings. However, I also saw others in more humble forms of transportation, and others had walked for days for the privilege of attending this wedding or just being near the immense celebration.

There were merchants setting up tents to cash in from the celebration. Everybody had a different type of journey to arrive at the feast of their lives. And suddenly I remembered Mother Mary's teachings on the meaning of this life's journey, which is to reach the light while being challenged by the distractions of the material realm.

Some of us take long roads, others find shortcuts, and others get distracted by the many roads and stop to sightsee; however, the destination is the same. We all want a fulfilling spiritual life. I finally understood clearly that the governor of the feast did not care to know where the good wine came from. He was happy that the problem had been solved.

Humans created the idea that there is only one way. Enlightenment is enlightenment, whether you got it from a corrupt preacher, an ascended spiritual master, a shaman high on magical herbs, on your own while walking through the woods—or even by being hit in the head with the Bible (sorry, this app is no longer available). But seriously, reaching the light is our common goal, and the road would definitely be less tragic if we practiced understanding and respect for one another's paths.

The Creator rejoices when even one of us reaches the light, and it is not a big deal how we accomplish this immense task. As long as we arrive at the light, he is totally thrilled that we got there. So the governor of the feast was thrilled that the best wine was produced and did not even ask who the source of the wine was. Jesus did not seem to mind either that the governor did not come to him; he addressed the groom instead. Once we are light, we are one with all there is, and taking credit is beyond the point.

After the good wine was presented to the governor, he said to the groom, "The good wine is served at the beginning, and when they are drunk, then the bad wine is served, but you have kept the best for later." One more riddle that succeeded in annoying me.

My guides, noticing my annoyance, proceeded to help me with the explanation. We were created by pure light as the best of the wines. We are born in light, not as pitiful sinners. (In Spanish, we have beautiful terminology for giving birth, which translates to "she gave light.") For one reason or another, most of us get confused and lost after the innocence of childhood and misplace our GPS. By losing our internal guiding system, we partake of the bad wine.

After transformation, our communication with the Creator gets better. Our internet is fast and clear; the joy of the good wine has arrived. We have tasted the sweetness of the marriage of heaven and earth, and we are equipped with a knowledge that is both liberating and blissful.

The story ends by saying that after the miracle, Jesus left with his brothers, mother, and disciples. This was somewhat puzzling also, as it seems that they left right after the miracle.

Again, I stopped writing for a few days to contemplate this statement and asked Mother Mary to give me her advice. Her answer totally stunned me. She said, "If you really have achieved transformation, you are the light. You are one with God. Literally, you don't need us anymore. The governor of the feast was directly speaking to the groom. You do not need an intermediary anymore."

I protested big-time. "But I still have work to do on my self-transformation, and I like having you and Jesus and my archangels and angels around."

She immediately calmed my fears and said, "We will always be your friends, because we understand that the human experience has many challenges. Our love is always with you, but you must believe that you are perfectly capable of going to the Creator directly. Jesus assured humanity that every one of you was special in the kingdom and capable of producing great miracles."

No wonder religions have kept the multitudes in the dark. It is big business selling salvation and feeding people bits of truth once in a while. These are the merchants I saw in the wedding feast vision, competing for a piece of the action. No more salvation on the installment plan for me.

I don't know what excited me more, discovering what salvation was or realizing that my Creator loves me unconditionally and that human perfection is an illusion. Imagine if we saw life as a huge wedding feast, which is what creation intended it to be. There is an abundance of great and interesting things at a wedding feast. There is great food, good wine, happy people dancing, and the expectation of great sex, not just for the bride and groom but for others who get inspired at weddings. There is also delicious gossip, happy and unhappy reunions, and the occasional fight of a few who drank a little too much of the bad wine.

Of course, if we party too much at the wedding feast, we might also have to deal with hangovers, upset stomachs, bill collectors, or unhappy in-laws, but such is life. Enjoy the good moments and accept and deal to the best of our ability with the challenging ones. We have to learn to forgive ourselves and others for mistakes and embrace it all in the knowledge that nothing is permanent.

The best part when we enter into this marriage is that spirit will never start divorce proceedings. The human part of us sometimes walks away, but the light is faithfully waiting for us with open arms. What an incredible partner—no fear, no jealousy, no judgment. Just infinite love.

I wish to remind my dear brothers and sisters that we came here to enjoy this beautiful plane of existence, like my dear Lady always tells me. We have let others influence our joy and peace of mind by misunderstood teachings and through brutal tactics to keep us in fear and guilt. Jesus took the earth mission to teach us how to live life without fear and suffocating rules. The God I know is pure love and wishes for us to enjoy every minute of our brief stop on earth. Play the game of life with enthusiasm and dignity, and you are contributing your share.

Jesus said, "If you are doing the will of the Father, you are my brother, my sister, my mother." If we are doing the best we can and we lovingly accept this earth mission, we are doing the will of the Father. Therefore, we are members of a great kingdom. Please believe that we have a complete heavenly family ready to assist us in creating a great life, but we also have the choice to find the stillness in ourselves and go directly to the light.

You are invited to celebrate life and enjoy creating and sharing. Let's enjoy our existence even if we find some bumps on the road and a few obnoxious wedding guests. And on the occasion that we have become the crazy wedding guest, let us learn from the lesson, forgive ourselves, and make contact again with the sustaining power of the light.

Let the wedding feast begin, and enjoy the marriage of heaven and earth. Light, love, and joy! And a glass of the best wine for the road!

AN EASY PLAN FOR AWAKENING AND TRANSFORMATION

I would like to work on a plan for enlightenment based on Jesus's true teachings of love. I believe in his teachings of love, not in the men's teaching of "Do as I say, or you will burn in hell." Any assistance you can give me will be greatly appreciated. I am concentrating on helping women, but let's design a plan that can be used by all.

"It is an honor to help you. We had ceremonies and practices that we followed according to his instructions. We will work on a plan that can help anybody start their own spiritual practice and open the path to enlightenment. The attributes we will work on are the building blocks of getting your being aligned to divine light and starting your road to a better life. This can be practiced by anybody at any level of ascension. The essence of his teaching is in the Bible; we will just clarify it better."

This is your way of making me read the Bible again.

"I am honored to help you understand the Bible better and to help you see clearly that his teachings were for unity and love for all. We will work on several attributes, as follows:

"*Faith*. The first thing you must realize is that you are a spark of divinity, made from divine substance, not from original sin. When you become aware of this truth, your faith in yourself and in the magnificence of the divine plan will sustain you every step of the way.

"*Wisdom*. By having faith in yourself and trusting in a divine plan, you become aware that intuition is your inheritance and the essence of your life's instruction manual. When the pathway of your intuition is clear, you have access to divine mind, where wisdom resides.

"*Strength.* Power comes from knowledge. When you know that you are divine light and that you have the wisdom to choose, then you are on your way to discovering your potential for powerful decisions and accomplishments.

"*Love.* By knowing that you are the light, just as the divine, and that everyone and everything contains the same light, you will remember infinite love. When you know that you come from infinite love, you are able to extend love to all.

"*Joy.* Sustainable joy comes from trusting in your divine master plan and executing it with faith, wisdom, strength, and love. Joy is automatic and sustainable when you know that you are supported by a great system that has your best interest in mind.

"When you have become one with the mentioned attributes, you will be excited to treat your body as a divine creation, to keep your mind in total awareness and your intuition aligned with the divine. Please understand what I have just said: *Your goal is to become faith, wisdom, strength, love, and joy. When you accomplish this, you are in our inner circle, and you have clear access to communication and inspiration. When you are in our inner circle, there is no fear or feelings of lack.*"

What about the ego and all its baggage? How do we get rid of fear and hate, and how do we forgive ourselves and others?

"Every one of these graces is accompanied by other graces. By staying on the plan, you will be adding virtues to your life and shedding unnecessary and painful baggage."

I think I get your point. If I am love, I am compassion; if I am compassion, I am forgiveness. If I am wisdom, I am abundance because I know how to create. If I am abundance, I am gratitude. If I am gratitude, I am joy, and so on.

"You see, my child, you have just reached another step on the enlightenment stairs. The way of the light is not difficult. It requires some commitment, but it should be enjoyable and accessible to all.

"After you implement the plan, your energy use becomes more efficient. You will be using your energy to expand love and will not waste it on fear or anxiety. You will be able to access your healing center faster and be able to collaborate with your doctors and healing practitioners when necessary."

I think I get your point. Using divine energy is then similar as the energy we use in our homes. We can use it wisely for our comfort, or we can waste it by letting it leak out by poor insulation and careless habits.

"You have made a perfect comparison. In other words, you will be insulating your being with the graces and dissolving bad habits and outdated thinking.

"Heaven will be with you every step of the way. Watch for the subtle signs, and be aware that some steps might be more difficult than others, but trust that with our guidance and your perseverance, success will be attained."

Thank you, dear Mother. I promise to do my best and stay with your instructions to the best of my ability. Please tell the angels that they will be working overtime.

I trust you, my dear Lady. Let's get to work. Help is on the way!

Awakening and Transformation Plan

"Keep a detailed journal of your thoughts, feelings, actions, and reactions. Pay attention to the little signs that the universe will be sending you. If possible, do the plan with others and gather with people who are also working on self-transformation.

"Every step will be practiced for a period of two days for a total of ten days. The eleventh day is for review, meditation, and contemplation. The twelfth day is for the wedding feast ritual."

Let me make sure that I understand this clearly. We will be working on the same attribute for two days. And we will go through the same meditation both days?

"That is correct, my dear. The first day is for the conscious mind to get used to a new way of thinking. The second day is for the subconscious mind to start working on clearing the pathways that are essential for the new plan for your life.

"Be in total knowing that this alignment is possible and easier than you think. Your intention is signaling the mind that you are ready. The special mantra and power statements will be your tools to assist you with your transformation.

"We will be working on steps one and two for ten days. You relax and reflect on the eleventh day, and the third step is taken on the wedding feast ritual. It is that simple. We are uniting the three aspects of mind. After the wedding feast ritual, you will be designing your new life.

"The power statements are to be repeated morning, noon, and night or any other time that you feel a disturbing emotion or thought taking over. Make sure to write all your power statements and the special mantra in bold letters. Keep your power statements accessible at all times.

"Do not fight your old thoughts. Tell them gently, '*You have served your purpose. It is time for ascension, and with the power of the light, I am now transforming you into loving energy to fuel my divine mission.*'"

Days 1 and 2—Faith

"Today you will start using the special and powerful mantra that communicates to the heavenly realms that you are ready for your new life. We are concentrating on the crown chakra at the top of your head.

"Speak your mantra with faith and strength. Mantras are a command to every cell of your body to listen and to create new pathways to a full and magical life. This mantra is your direct message to the universe that transformation is desired, and by the power of these words, you are claiming your divine right to your best life.

"*I believe with all my being that I am faith.*

"*I believe with all my mind that I am wisdom.*

"*I believe with all my spirit that I am strength.*

"*I believe with all my heart that I am love.*

"*I believe with all my soul that I am joy.*

"The special mantra is to be repeated as soon as you get up in the morning the first eleven days of the plan.

"Start the day with the special mantra given above. Then proceed with the meditation for the day."

Days 1 and 2—Meditation for Faith

"During meditation, imagine the golden light of creation surrounding and guiding you every minute of your existence on this earth. This soothing light enters your body through your crown chakra (top of your head) and illuminates every cell of your body. Create a feeling of total faith in this infinite light, knowing that you are a precious receptor of this light. Enjoy this beautiful feeling during your meditation and carry this feeling with you now and forever.

"With a clear and strong voice, declare your powerful statements for the day.

"*I am faith, and I am confident that my life has a divine purpose. My sacred, personal mission is to bring light and love to the world.*

"If you have been waiting for a particular outcome of any situation, write on your journal the results that you would like to experience. Ask the angels to assist you in achieving this experience because you now know that this is for your highest good and the good of humanity. While praying or meditating, imagine and feel that you deserve to receive such an experience. Believe that your life's divine script is within you and that you are taking the right steps to recover those memories and realize your true life. Trust that you have a spiritual support system ready to assist you.

"Remind yourself often that faith in the Creator means faith in yourself also. Believe that you are an important component of creation and that your sacred mission is unfolding and expanding along with your faith."

Days 3 and 4—Wisdom

"You become wisdom by having faith in yourself and living your life from a position of alignment with source. Please realize that every human being is equipped with intuition, and it is always with you. Your intuition has been partially dormant for some time, but you are now on the correct road to clearing your pathway. You were born with your intuition pathway in clear condition and perfect working order, and the sooner you recover this gift, the better your life will become. Our work for wisdom centers in clearing your third eye chakra, the middle point between your eyebrows.

"You get reacquainted with your intuition by visualization, journaling, and paying attention to your dreams. It also helps to be watchful of the synchronicities of life. Breathing correctly is the best tool for keeping your intuition aligned to source. When you master your breath, it becomes easier to integrate every aspect of your being.

"Your assignment for this step is to pay attention to your breath and to flood your being with the power of life contained in each breath. You will also concentrate on visualizing your new life. Be extremely creative and use your power of visualization to see yourself in the life that you always knew you could have. Know that there are powerful forces seen and unseen collaborating with your new intentions.

"Also know that this is the time for all those dreams and special projects to become reality. They will become reality because now you have the correct guiding system. Your dreams are our dreams, and they become reality when you know this truth. We are your most devoted cheering section, because we know that life on the earth plane requires great inner strength and dedication."

Days 3 and 4—Meditation for Wisdom

"Visualizing is a powerful component for your new life. Become comfortable by being aware of your inhalations and exhalations. During meditation, start visualizing a beautiful and peaceful scene outdoors. It can be the ocean, mountains, or your favorite park.

"See yourself finding a comfortable spot and sitting on the ground, feeling one with the earth. See yourself surrounded by all the beautiful gifts of nature—animals, flowers, trees, fresh air, and so on. Call in the assistance of your favorite animal and ask for help in getting acquainted with your intuition. Imagine that you know the workings of nature just as this beautiful companion does. Stay a few minutes in this serene environment and let go of worries and pain.

"Visualize that you now possess the inner compass that can help you feel comfortable in your physical body while being guided by spirit. Enjoy every detail of this beautiful scene and know that from now on you can meet your nature friends in this peaceful and wise place. Write in your journal a detailed description of your visit and go about your day noticing the wonder of nature and all those free gifts of flowers and beauty.

"Your power statements for this stage are the following: *With every breath I take, I am clearing the pathway of my intuition. I am wisdom. I am aware of the signs and opportunities for my new life. My divine plan is unfolding with clarity and joy.*

"Write clear questions in your journal and feel safe in the knowledge that they will be answered. Be aware of the little signs and synchronicities that will start appearing in your daily life.

"Before going to sleep, ask divine wisdom to assist you in your dream time with the answers that you seek. Keep a dream journal and write down any dream that you remember, even if at the moment it seems insignificant. With practice, you will be amazed at how easy it is to access your precious gift of intuition."

Day 5 and 6 Are for Working on Strength

"Your assignment for this step is to write your own power statements and declare them aloud with conviction and certainty. Know that you are a vessel of strength, and from now on, you intend to take advantage of your inner power. During this step, you are clearing your voice area (throat chakra). Clear communication is an essential tool for your new life.

"Make a decision that you deserve to be heard and that you have great ideas to share with the world. This is very important because most children are raised with mistaken practices oppressing their voices and opinions."

Meditation for Strength

"Before meditation, say your power statements out loud with authority and create the feeling that the words penetrate every cell of your body. During meditation, feel the unity that is taking place in your entire being and know that you possess spiritual and physical strength. Feel the power of divine light clearing blockages from your throat area and replacing them with inner strength to voice your opinions, ideas, and desires. Feel the love of Divine Mother merging with the strength of the Creator, gifting you with a beautiful infusion of inner courage and unconditional love. This powerful combination creates the feeling that your voice is attractive and unique and a very important component for your new life.

"As you go about your day, face people and situations with courage and trusting that you are in control, armed with faith, wisdom, and strength. If you have been putting off dealing with a situation or completing a challenging task, this is the time to begin using your inner strength. Plan your success strategy and follow it to completion. Feel gratitude for your voice that lets you communicate your desires to the universe and humanity.

"Speak your truth and state your ideas clearly. Feel strong in the knowledge that every word you speak is full of your truth and wisdom. Know that you are capable of setting boundaries. Plan to teach others to respect your space and your ideas. Become aware of your language patterns and use compassionate and uplifting words for yourself and others. Words have immense power. Use your power wisely. Be in gratitude for your own unique voice and enjoy the power of the spoken word."

Days 7 and 8 Are for Working on Love

"During this stage, we are working on remembering love. Love is always present. However, many times it is masked by attachments and addictions. You were created out of infinite love; therefore, you are love and will remain love eternally. At this stage, we are working with our heart energy center, also known as the fourth chakra."

Meditation for Love

"Imagine that the love of Divine Mother is at the center of your heart. Feel the warm feeling that this love produces. Envelop yourself with this love and merge it with the light of the Father that is entering your body through your crown chakra. Feel peaceful and secure. Peace comes from knowing that you are cherished by an intelligent and divine system. Enjoy this bliss and know that you have access to it always. Know that fear has been transformed to love. Feel safe in this pure love and see some of this powerful essence healing every cell of your body. Share some of this loving essence with your family, friends, and the planet. Your power statements for this stage are as follows:

I am creating my new life from the love of my heart and magnifying love for my benefit and the benefit of humanity. My sacred mission is my treasure, and this mission is surrounded with the love of my heart.

"Jesus said, 'For where your treasure is there will your heart be also.' He was speaking about keeping your sacred mission in the love of your heart to create out of love. When you create out of love, you are utilizing powerful energy vibrations from the physical heart and the love center of your light body. This is a powerful and unstoppable combination.

"Practice love by being kind and loving to yourself first. This step is extremely important. Love yourself, forgive yourself, and vanish judgment and guilt.

"Please be extremely kind to yourself and be firm in the belief that to love others, you need to start with your own beautiful and special being. Admire your talents, and believe me, you have countless talents. Give yourself time to be alone and get to know the real you. Congratulate yourself for having made the decision to discover the light within.

"Learn to give love from the overflow of your cup and keep abundant reserves for yourself. Teach others to unite with love so their cups can overflow too. If every heart was overflowing with love, transformation would be instantaneous for the entire planet. All the instructions for an abundant life are contained in Psalm 23. Please pay attention. Your cup is meant to be running over always.

"After you are convinced that you have become love and that the Creator loves you unconditionally, you can begin with showing others the way of love and compassion. You can start with small acts of kindest, but with time, your acts of love will become greater and greater, because you are now serving others from your heart and generating love from the never-ending supply. You are giving effortlessly because you know how to receive now. You are giving love from the constant flow of the light, not from a place of sacrifice. When you give from love, you also receive from love. Enjoy the experience of receiving and giving.

"During your daily activities, be grateful to yourself for performing your work and your daily chores with love. Be in the knowing that the job you are doing is adding love and compassion to your world, whether you are washing a child's hands or making international deals. Your loving actions are greatly appreciated by the unifying light of creation."

Days 9 and 10 Are for Working on Joy

"By now, you are feeling better, your practice is developing, and you are beginning to see changes. Joy, like love, is one of the gifts you were born with. I know what you are thinking. *How can we be joyful with all the bad news and cruelty going on in the world these days?* Please remember that joy is your divine right. You have to reclaim it and become joy. Less evolved beings will be doing what less evolved beings do, but do not let them do more destroying by allowing them to steal your joy. Do your part in lessening their destruction by staying in joy and sharing your strategies with those suffering.

"It is in your best interest to realize that being in physical form is just a mission that you gladly accepted and that you will certainly return home eventually. Imagine planning and going on a trip and not enjoying it because of some unexpected mishaps."

Meditation for Joy

"Use your imagination to create a wonderful ceremony where the angels or your favorite ascended master hands you the gift of joy. Feel this gift of joy surrounding you and make the choice to accept it and treasure it. Capture the feeling of joy and happiness in your solar plexus energy center and carry it with you through every activity of your life. As you go about your day, do things that will make you happy and adopt a childlike attitude.

"Enjoy the little and the big pleasures of life. Spend time in the company of people who love to laugh. Children joyfully go about their day, changing games and best friends without looking back and regretting any decision. This is what Jesus meant when he said the kingdom of heaven belongs to the children. If you stay as joyful as a child, you are in the kingdom of heaven, creating and advancing and leaving behind habits that do not serve you anymore. Your power statements will make you feel as happy and joyful as a child.

"I am reclaiming my gift of joy. I came to the earth playground to enjoy creating. I give myself permission to play and enjoy the game of life.

"Do not let anybody or anything steal your joy. When a situation arises that can steal your joy, declare your power statements with strength and conviction."

Day 11 Is to Review Your Progress and Ask Spirit to Help You Meet Your Guides and Angels

"Every human being is born with all the help she/he will need on the journey, but it is up to the individual to ask for guidance. There is an army of angels waiting for your every order, including your guardian angel. There are also ascended masters ready to help. Make sure that you ask for help, no matter how insignificant the problem. It is just a matter of getting used to asking. It is your right to ask, and it is our privilege to assist you.

"Today is a day for reflection, prayer, and meditation. Ask for help in identifying your angels and guides. If you were acquainted with a special ascended being or angel in childhood, state that you want him/her in your life again. It is that easy; just ask and know that they are at your service. Review your journal and note your new insights.

"This is also a good day to clean your personal space and clear your house of unnecessary clutter.

"Plan and enjoy your day. Work in your garden, take a walk, or read a favorite book. Do the activities that make you feel connected to nature and spirit."

Day 12—Wedding Feast Ceremony

"Time this ceremony for a weekend or day off. Be in the moment and enjoy every step of your beautiful ceremony. You will need the following:

- six ounces of good, clean water in a glass container
- your best crystal glass or pottery cup (no plastic please)
- one candle of your choice in a safe glass container (a battery candle is fine too)
- white, clean clothes

"Today you will nourish your being with the transforming and healing power of water. Start your day by taking a shower and appreciate the cleansing power of water. Imagine that past regrets and mistakes are going down the drain and to the earth to be transformed into goodness for all. Talk loudly and clearly to all your fears and insecurities. Tell them that their time is up and send them down with the command to be transformed into healing energies for Mother Earth. If you never sing in the shower, today is the day to start. Rejoice in the new, confident you. Sing with strength and joy.

"After showering, dress in your clean white clothes. Place the items on your altar or coffee table. Put on your favorite soft music.

"Light the candle and invite your guides and angels to be with you.

"Spend a few minutes observing the light of the candle to clear your mind.

"Pour the water into your special cup or glass and enjoy a feeling of gratitude.

"Repeat the transformation mantra below with conviction, excitement, and strength. If you do not resonate with the beings of light mentioned in the mantra, call on the beings you are comfortable with. Transformation is celebrated by all.

Transformation Mantra
By the light of infinite Father,
the love of Divine Mother,
and the transforming power of water,
I celebrate the union of every aspect of myself.
I am united, I am loved, I am complete.
I am one with the light and love of Christ.

"Raise your glass to the heavens in a special celebration of unity and love.

"Drink the water slowly and know that every center of energy and every cell of your body is being purified and united with the light.

"Contemplate the flame of the candle for a few minutes and know that this light represents the light that is within you.

"Extinguish the candle and keep it on your altar as a remembrance of the light that is always inside you.

"Go about your day loving every aspect of your yourself and appreciating the new you.

"You have partaken of the wedding feast ceremony and have blended spirit and flesh for a harmonious and sweet honeymoon for the rest of your life.

"You have now completed the plan. Your conscious mind is clear and aligned with your subconscious mind, and you can access universal mind. You are now ready to start using your new gifts to create the magical life that you always wanted. When Jesus shared the bread and wine at the last supper, he was affirming his commitment to assist humanity in the marriage of matter and spirit. Be happy, dear ones, and share the love and joy with others."

After I completed the plan, I was advised by Mother Mary to change the special mantra from believing to knowing, and she explained to me that Jesus performed his miracles by knowing totally that he was one with God. The key to miracles is in knowing without the shadow of a doubt that you are a vessel of divine wisdom and light.

I know with all my being that I am faith.
I know with all my mind that I am wisdom.
I know with all my spirit that I am strength.
I know with all my heart that I am love.
I know with all my soul that I am joy.
I am faith.
I am wisdom.
I am strength.
I am love.
I am joy.

The shorter version will work also.

Meditation to Assist You In Creating Your New Life

"You have now claimed your divinity, and you are invited to the most sacred meditation space, where you will be assisted with your new experience."

Welcome to the Reunion of Heaven and Earth

Start your meditation as you usually do, and after you feel relaxed, imagine walking through a beautiful meadow full of the most colorful flowers and amazing vegetation. As you slowly walk, the colors get more vivid and attractive. You see countless butterflies and birds of every color. As you advance through this amazing field of beauty, you are feeling more relaxed with every breath you take. The freshness of the air is healing and revitalizing every cell of your body. You are enjoying every minute of this transforming experience hosted by your loving Mother Earth. You walk slowly, feeling safe and mesmerized by all this peace and beauty, and as you take a few more steps, you realize that you are getting closer and closer to the mountains, and you know that this road brings you to more magic and love. You notice that the tallest mountain has a golden door, and your intuition is guiding you to walk through this immense opening and receive your gifts from Mother Earth. The inside of this mountain is a resting place for your mind, body, and soul.

There are ancestors and healers ready to assist you with every need that you ever had. As you walk inside, you are welcomed by a wise and loving medicine woman. She will be your guide and healer for this journey. You see many happy people who have found healing, joy, and laughter. This loving medicine woman tells you that you are totally loved and treasured. She takes you by the hand and brings you to a space of immense beauty and rest. There are tables set up with healing waters and bountiful fruits and herbs. You find a comfortable place to sit on the ground and recline on a soft and comfortable cushion. She also sits on the ground facing you and calls for a helper to bring healing herbs, water, and fruits. Her hands work fast, infusing the water with the energy of the herbs and fruits. She offers you a cup of this refreshing water. As you drink it, you realize that this blessed liquid has the power of healing and balancing your life. Gratitude is flowing all through your body and mind, and you know that life is worth living, and the small and simple pleasures are rich gifts to be enjoyed with total awareness and love. She lovingly tells you that Mother Earth has always been ready to shower you with abundance of health and love. The loving energy emanating from this loving medicine woman is surrounding you, and you know that from this day forward, you will do your best to enjoy the blessings that Mother Nature provides. You become aware of the need to preserve these blessings for new arrivals to our loving and bountiful planet. You continue resting and enjoying this amazing space and feel the embrace of all this beauty and peace. You are aware of the unity with Mother Earth and know that she loves you and wishes to provide comfort and simplicity for you.

After a few minutes of this total communion with comfort and peace, you slowly get up to continue your journey. Your guide gently guides you to another healing space, down a few steps, where you see people gathering by a beautiful lake with powerful healing waters. They are dipping their hands in the water and discharging everything that is no longer needed. Your intuition tells you to let the water take all your fears and worries. You scan your body for feelings of fear and insecurity, gather them in your hands, and proceed to discharge them in the water of transformation. You can feel the healing power of the water penetrating your hands and entire body. What a relief; you feel lighter and peaceful. You have just surrendered not only your heavy burdens but also those inherited from past generations. You are now a clean and joyful vessel of light and love. Feeling gratitude for all your ancestors and teachers, you proceed to go in the direction of the exit. You know that you are now a new person and you have left fear and lack behind.

Your benevolent guide tells you that she will take you to your next destination, which is the Crystal Pyramid, where you will find the Temple of Light and the Altar of Infinite Love. You walk happily and joyfully with this beautiful being, and within a few minutes, you can see the impressive Crystal Pyramid. As you get closer, you can see angels and beings of light singing and playing by the outdoor fountains. The pyramid emanates mesmerizing light and soothing sound that envelops your entire being. While enjoying this new experience, you can see Divine Mother coming to greet you. Your grandmotherly guide lovingly introduces you to Divine Mother and says her goodbyes. You feel so special and loved, and you are definitely ready for the next phase of your journey and the company of Divine Mother. Her eyes are full of compassion and love, and you can feel all this love in every cell of your body. You are literally merging with unconditional love. You are guided inside this incredible pyramid. The beauty of the inside is beyond your wildest dreams. Every angle is full of light, and you can feel this light taking up residency in your entire body. As you walk hand in hand with Divine Mother, she takes you to the center of the pyramid to the Temple of Light. This is an amazing temple where all the prayers and petitions of humanity are received and lovingly accepted. There is infinite trust in this loving and illuminating temple, and you know that everything is as it should be and that every prayer is answered for your highest good. Divine Mother now takes you to the center of the Temple of Light for a special reunion with infinite love. At the center of the Temple of Light, you see a multicolor altar with several levels radiating pure, infinite love. You are dazzled by all this beauty and color, and slowly you see five levels to this altar.

Divine Mother invites you to the top of the altar to sit and enjoy all this beauty. You absorb all this light and beauty and realize that you are being presented with the five virtues of your divine plan. Divine Mother is transferring to you the gift of faith, and you repeat after her the special mantra, as follows: *I know with all my being that I am faith.* You can feel the transformation in every level of your light bodies, as well as your physical body.

After this special moment, you both descend one step, and you can see that you have another gift waiting. This time, she transfers to you the gift of wisdom. She lovingly touches your forehead and hands you this precious gift of wisdom, and you repeat after her, *I know with all my mind that I am wisdom.*

Slowly you descend another step, and now you are in possession of your third gift, which is strength. She smiles at you and tells you that you have always been strong and capable of thriving and succeeding in every path that your heart desires. You smile back and pronounce your affirmation with power and certainty: *I know with all my spirit that I am strength.*

With great optimism and hope, you descend to the next step. Now she is transferring to you her very special gift of love. You can feel this love coming directly from her heart to yours. This feeling is beyond description, and now you understand that love is everything. Love also brings unity, and suddenly you feel one with all there is. What a beautiful feeling of freedom and rest. No more heavy burdens to carry. Everything is in divine order, and life is flowing with ease and happiness. You now repeat, *I know with all my heart that I am love.*

Enjoying all this love, you both descend the last step of this beautiful Altar of Love, and she is now gifting you with joy, which is just a formality, because your entire being is now in total joy. You can hear angels laughing and singing, and you understand that this is how life is supposed to flow. With immense gratitude, you affirm the last part of the mantra, *I know with all my soul that I am joy.*

Divine Mother is just as joyful, and she embraces you in her loving arms and whispers to you her final blessing: "Go in peace, my child. You are always in my heart. Be the love that the world needs and enjoy every instant of your precious life. I am grateful for your efforts to seek the light. I am forever with you."

You stay quiet and silent for the next few minutes and slowly feel your being back in the earth realm. You are so grateful for this experience and eager to apply all the gifts you have received to your new life. Give yourself a big hug and admire your soul for taking the steps to live your life with spiritual integrity and love. With gratitude and compassion, go about your day, knowing that you are special and totally loved. Remember your new gift as follows: *I am faith, I am wisdom, I am strength, I am love, I am joy.*

For the next few weeks, you will be adjusting to your new way of thinking. It takes approximately forty days for all aspects to develop harmony.

Please be aware that issues will be coming up, but stay true to your new purpose, and success will be yours.

Start taking action by researching the new projects that you have in mind. If you always wanted to write a book, get educated about the process and set a date to start writing. If you want to change your life by changing locations, do the same; start researching places of interest, make phone calls to employment prospects, and so on. Remember, it is a marriage of heaven and earth. Spirit will guide, and the physical body needs to be in action. There is no more time to be spiritually or physical lazy. Enjoy your new adventure.

As you continue with your daily spiritual practice, please make sure to practice the virtues as follows:

Meditate and reflect on each attribute each day, starting with faith on Mondays and finishing with joy on Fridays. Repeat the part of the special mantra that goes with each attribute. For example, on Monday, you say, "I know with all my being that I am wisdom," and so on with the rest of the weekdays.

On Saturdays, be aware and grateful for Mother Earth and the material plane. Enjoy being in nature or working in your garden. Be grateful for your material blessings. Always remember that we are meant to be abundant in every aspect of our lives. Money, when used properly, adds joy and freedom to our lives. We have to think of money as part of us; there is no separation between us and money, just like there is no separation between us and the divine. I will share some of my favorite affirmations, but you may create your own.

Well-being and prosperity are with me always, and I share joyfully.

Money comes into my life with the fluidity of water hydrating my body.

I know with every cell of my body that I am advancing daily to great spiritual and financial accomplishments.

My everlasting talents support me and allow me great riches and strength.

Please know that these are no ordinary affirmations; my guides have helped me choose words that speak directly to our communication towers. Have fun asking your guides to download powerful words to create your own mantras.

On Sundays, place a glass of water on your altar before meditation, and after your spiritual practice, thank the water for your daily transformation and drink the water with gratitude and joy. These small rituals will train your mind to stay on the enlightenment track always.

The affirmation for Sundays is based on the overall essence of the plan: *I love myself with all my heart, with all my soul, with my entire mind, and with all my strength.*

My Experience with the Plan

In order to learn the plan and teach it to others, I was advised by my Lady to do the plan during Lent. I dedicated several days to each attribute, then reflected for several days. I did the wedding feast ritual on Easter Sunday. We then decided to shorten it for busy lives and agreed on twelve days. However, it is up to each individual to make it fit your particular schedule. If you are Catholic, you can choose to wait for Lent or any other important date. If you are a follower of another path or religion, you can choose to include a date that it is meaningful to you. Be creative and know that there is no right or wrong way for transformation, only opportunities to advance your way to the light.

Mother Mary explained that your old nature will sometimes make a valiant effort to resurface. This is why the mantra is changed from belief to knowing. Our old nature needed to believe, and while it is still good to believe, our new nature is all-knowing because it is now centered in love and guided by spirit. When we know that we are an important guest at the wedding feast, then we are powerful beyond belief.

My biggest struggle while doing the plan was with strength, but it will be different with everybody. Having cultivated a relationship with my heavenly buddies since childhood, I had no major problems with the other attributes. Because of childhood diseases and the home environment I was raised in, I grew up thinking that I was weak in inner and outer strength. During those weeks, every situation that could test my strength was presented to me. And in the moments that I became weak, my joy also diminished.

I enlisted the help of an entire group of angels. I kept the unemployment rates at all-time lows in heaven all by myself. But I am happy to say that the breakthroughs came just in time. I have gained confidence and power to tell people the truth when they are annoying me and to tell others to leave my space when necessary. I had the strength to walk away from people and situations that were not adding anything positive to my life and to come to terms as to why I needed such lessons.

I was able to understand my parents better and to know that our sacred contracts were designed with my spiritual growth in mind. I was able to laugh with my mother about what I called my boot camp upbringing, but she reminded me that she mellowed out in her old age and turned into a sweet and wise grandmother, adored by her many grandchildren. I am honored to be her daughter and grateful for all the advice that she has passed on to me.

She also mentioned that she had always admired my inner strength, which was news to me. And she reminded me that only a strong person would have the courage to get on an airplane at the age of eighteen for another country, armed only with a suitcase and few hundred dollars. Amen.

I have a routine that I have developed to keep my body, mind, and soul in optimal working conditions. Your success will depend on your determination, action, and perseverance. I start my day with the affirmation for the day and thanking the angels and my guides for a new day. I also thank my body for being the house of my spirit and tell myself that I intend to nourish and hydrate my body properly this day. After following the transformation plan, your body's needs will change, and old, harmful habits will disappear. I eat smaller amounts now, and my body totally rejects red meats and instead craves fruits and vegetables. My lifelong problems with anemia and fatigue are under control, even though I no longer eat red meat.

I do yoga or tai chi or my own shamanic dance for at least twenty minutes. If the weather is good, I replace yoga with walking. If you don't have twenty minutes, even five minutes daily is better than no practice at all. If you don't practice any form of exercise, just moving to beautiful music will signal your body to feel joy and start the day on good vibrations.

After my daily exercise, I find it easier to do my meditation. I usually do twenty minutes. I used to think that in order to get any benefits, I had to meditate for hours. While I still like long meditations, just for the pleasure of it, any amount of time is highly effective and will get the mind used to the daily routine. I also meditate at night for a few minutes for better sleep.

After you adopt a daily routine, you will be amazed at the difference it will make in your life. You will find yourself quieting your mind in busy places and just observing life, which is another form of meditation. You will enjoy and contemplate nature more and fall in love with your life and the universe.

By taking care of your complete being, you become healthier, content, and ready to plan a brighter and more fulfilling life. It becomes easier to work on the body and adopt a well-being plan when you have connected with spirit. One gift that I give to myself is having a professional massage often. My body loves it and responds by cooperating beautifully with my healing.

Life will always present its challenges, but you are better prepared to deal with them. Your internal joy cannot be taken away by a situation or a less evolved human being. I often find myself now offering very little resistance to perceived challenges and problems because I am in the knowing that I am protected and encouraged by a divine system that has my well-being in mind.

If I lose my patience or offend somebody, I recognize that I am not running for the Ms. Perfect title. I excuse and forgive myself first. I also find the humor or the lesson in the situation and congratulate myself for the wisdom to see things clearly. And more importantly, I am now quick to apologize to the person I have offended. I am also better prepared to accept apologies from others, and I quickly clear bad feelings and offenses out of my system.

I still struggle with the injustices of the world, and I get sad when I see others suffering, but I bring myself quickly into alignment again and remind myself that there are many mysteries that I don't understand yet and that each soul is traveling at its own pace and timing. I also remind myself that it is better to stay strong in order to help myself and others.

The biggest insight I have discovered after doing the plan has been to attain a feeling of finally belonging. It is such a relief to feel at ease with my virtues and imperfections. I now feel comfortable in any group and in any situation, knowing that I am genuine and that I don't have to pretend that I am perfect. I love myself and enjoy my moments of insanity and brilliance equally. I am me; take her or leave her. I will be fine either way. My beloved brothers and sisters of the light, do I hear a big amen!

Helpful Techniques

Learning to Meditate

If you have never meditated, practice for at least three weeks before starting the awakening and transformation plan. Become aware of your breathing pattern and learn techniques to change to a healthier breathing system. There are professionals who can help you retrain your breath, or you can find information in books and videos. In my opinion, the practice of yoga is the best way to learn breathwork and work on your body at the same time.

Meditation has become more popular in the last few years, and we are finally realizing that being in silence and daily accessing our divine reservoir of wisdom and love is beneficial and necessary for our well-being. I have practiced and taught meditation for many years, even when people thought it was some kind of weird practice. There are many paths to achieving a quiet mind, and I will do my best to explain my technique and make it as easy as possible.

The most important step is *intention*. Write in your journal that from this day forward, you intend to access the silence where all the answers reside.

After intention comes *action*. Make a plan with a starting date and prepare the space where you will meditate. If you wish to join a meditation group, write your desire in your journal and ask your inner guiding system to help you find a group where you will fit in and enjoy the company of others of like mind.

Last but not least, *perseverance*. Make the commitment to give yourself the gift of a few minutes every day dedicated to your spiritual practice. This is part of loving yourself and becoming aware that by starting with yourself, you will be better equipped to help others. Self-love is the key to helping yourself and eventually becoming the guiding light for others.

After you have decided on the space that you will use, prepare your altar with images of ascended masters, angels, crystals, candles, and so on. This will be the space where you not only meditate but where you listen to beautiful music and talk to your angels and guides. This will also be the space where you place your written petitions to the universe and where you perform the wedding feast ritual.

Since my main guide is Mother Mary, she is prominent in my altar, but I also have Jesus, Buddha, angels, special gifts from loved ones, and candles. A pyramid is extremely beneficial to have on your altar.

With time, the energy of your little corner will become an incredible sacred space of peace, love, and oneness with the divine.

I love putting fresh flowers on my altar, and those flowers last for weeks just from the energy of my little sacred space. If you decide to start meditating on your own, the following steps will be helpful:

Decide ahead of time how many minutes you will dedicate to your practice. Be generous with yourself, but do not feel bad if you can only find a few minutes each day. Even a few minutes a day will make a big difference in calming your mind for the rest of the day. I will assume that we are working with twenty minutes.

The first five minutes are for your body. Do some type of gentle yoga, tai chi, or easy dance steps. Be aware of your breath and imagine every inhalation bringing you peace and every exhalation sending peace to the world. This step is necessary to relax the body and to signal the mind to cooperate.

The next ten minutes are for your mind. If noise is a problem, play relaxing or meditating music.

Sit comfortably with spine straight—feet touching the floor, hands on your lap, palms up, eyes closed.

Interlace your fingers and have the tips of your thumbs touching. I like my hands touching to be on notice that the final goal is integration of all the aspects of me.

Choose two words that resonate with you for your breathwork. I use *love* and *grace*.

As you slowly inhale, imagine that the love of the Father is cleansing every cell of your being, and as you exhale, imagine that the grace of the

Mother is magnifying love in every cell of your body, in your sacred space, and in the entire earth.

Concentrate on observing your breath inhaling love and exhaling grace. Do not force your breath. Slowly you will get comfortable with deeper breaths. It took years to acquire the unhealthy habit of shallow breathing; therefore, it will take time to develop a new habit of correct breathing. This is the most important step in my opinion. People give up because they feel that they cannot retrain their breathing system. Please be extremely patient and compassionate with yourself. Your body knows and will cooperate with healthy, new habits. It is difficult for negative thoughts to invade your mind when you are concentrating on your breath and enjoying the beautiful energy of love and grace. If thoughts persist in entering this sacred silence, do not fight them; share the love and grace. Feel comfortable in the enjoyment of peace. Eventually, the space between thoughts will become greater and greater. You will cherish the silence, and new insights will appear in your daily life. With patience and perseverance, you will start experiencing glimpses of oneness and bliss, which are the highest rewards for your dedication.

The last five minutes are for unity of mind, body, soul, and spirit. Slowly rub your hands together and place them on your solar plexus center. Imagine that by meditating daily, your conscious mind is in agreement with your subconscious mind and together will access the infinite mind where all the answers exist. Imagine merging wisdom with love and knowing that this combination of divine ingredients will guide you to your transformation and the life you were meant to live.

Spend these last few minutes in prayer or conversation with the heavenly guides and thank them for assisting you in this wonderful new adventure. Bring your awareness to your body. Slowly move your fingers and toes. Put your hands in prayer position and bring them to your heart. When you feel comfortable, slowly open your eyes and feel comfort in the fact that you are always surrounded by divine light and unconditional love. Also thank Mother Earth for keeping you grounded in her loving energy. Last but not least, thank yourself for taking the steps to ascension.

Do not worry about the exact timing of each step; your intuition will guide you through every stage, and with practice, it becomes automatic as to how many minutes you need to enjoy in each stage.

Your individual practice is very important, but it is also rewarding to find a meditating group where you can share experiences and learn from others. Practice mindfulness throughout your day. When a thought of fear or despair comes in, acknowledge the thought, breathe in love, and breathe out grace. Gently transform it into a thought of love and trust. Remember, a thought is energy. Do not suppress it or send it out to add to the pile of toxic thoughts floating around in the aura of our planet; instead, transform it by love and sent it out joyfully.

May you have many blessings and beautiful moments of divine silence.

Dancing to Cleanse Emotions

I love energy dancing and often experiment with different types of music and create my own rituals. I like shamanic or uplifting music for cleansing toxic thoughts and emotions.

Play your favorite music. Tell yourself aloud that it is time to have fun and enjoy moving your body and clearing your energy.

Relax and feel the music entering every cell of your body, dancing slowly for a few minutes.

Lift your arms above your head and imagine the angels gently placing a ball of pure, brilliant light in your hands.

Dance slowly, bringing the ball of light from the top of your head to the rest of your body, moving slowly to the music. Cleanse your body with this energy and imagine past hurts and any type of toxic emotion attaching to the ball of light like a magnet collects objects. Imagine every cell of your body becoming healthy and happy. Enjoy every step and every dance move like a professional dancer does.

After you have cleansed every cell of your body, give the energy to Mother Earth by imagining that the ball of light is going out of your hands and burying itself in the ground. Ask Mother Earth to convert your discarded emotions and past traumas into clean energy and well-being for the good of all. Relax and imagine the energy of unconditional love keeping your aura totally clear and ready to protect your emotions and thoughts.

Meditation to Undo Sacred Contracts

When a pattern keeps repeating in our lives and we cannot find any explanation, it usually means that it has a past-life connection or an inherited ancestry pattern. In any case, those agreements and unwanted traits can be undone by intention and meditation. You don't have to identify if it is a past-life connection, a too ambitious soul curriculum, or a family pattern. Just make sure that you are convinced that you do not want to experience those difficulties anymore.

Write in your journal the repeating pattern and the damage that it has done to your life and in some cases to the lives of others. State that from this day forward, this pattern will be terminated because it is the best thing to do for your highest good and the good of humanity.

Start your meditation as usual. When you feel comfortable and relaxed, ask your favorite angel or ascended master to open up your book of sacred contracts. If there are other people involved in your repeating pattern, you may invite their higher selves to be present at this ceremony. Assure them that this is being done with love and for the progress of all concerned. It you are not comfortable inviting others' higher selves, that is fine too; it will work either way. Divine wisdom is all-knowing and all-loving.

Picture a beautiful white book with golden letters. Open the book and find the necessary contract and ask the master that you have chosen as your assistant to drop nine drops of wisdom on this page, erasing the lesson from this life's experience.

Imagine a lavender healing oil and see the nine drops falling one by one and deleting the lesson along with the suffering. See the page become empty and clean. Rejoice in the knowledge that it is done.

Now that the page is clean, picture yourself writing your new sacred contract. Be creative and specific with everything you desire. Sign your new sacred contract and ask the ascended being to sign as a witness to your new contract. It is very important to date your new contract.

Rejoice in the knowledge that it is done. If you had invited others' higher selves, thank them for being present and tell them that from this day forward, the slate is clean and everything is forgiven. Dismiss them with love and compassion and wish them the best of life always.

Come out of your meditation as you normally do, slowly and joyfully. Write your experience of the ceremony in your journal and be in the knowing that you have received because you have asked.

Stay with a joyful feeling all through the day and keep congratulating yourself for writing your new contract and a new vision for a better life.

Use the same ceremony for redesigning sacred agreements with parents, children, or relatives, but instead of terminating the entire contract, you can undo the difficult parts and create new joyful and healing clauses for the benefit of all.

I was given this ritual when I had a difficult situation at work. I was considering walking away from my employer because of an envious coworker. But the situation was healed, and I could continue in daily dealings with the other individual with no negative consequences. When the right time came, I left the employment due to my desire to explore and grow. The nine drops mean triple strength of healing for mind, body, and soul.

My Daily Facelift

After ending my daily meditation routine, I pay special attention to my face. This is also a good practice while working on the love step of the plan. This helps with loving ourselves and discovering our own beauty.

Look in the mirror and tell yourself that Divine Mother loves you unconditionally and that you are a reflection of her own beauty and love. Rub your hands together for a slow count of twenty-one.

Place both hands close to your face and imagine divine love and energy giving vitality and beauty to every cell of your face. Imagine your facial skin renovating itself with every breath and radiating joy and beauty. Lightly touch any perceived imperfections or problem areas; give love to those areas and tell your cells to be vibrant and beautiful, and thank them for acting on your commands. Affirm daily that you are beauty and you radiate beauty.

Beauty to me is a genuine smile, a peaceful mind, and accepting the marks of time with grace and gratitude. When we discover our own beauty, we see beauty in every aspect of creation.

Of course, if we ever need a little work from a skilled surgeon, we will bless her and be grateful for her talent and creation.

Morning Wake-Up Call

As soon as I wake up, I give thanks to my angels for having kept me and my family safe. I give thanks to my own being for the strength and wisdom that will be used to face the day. While saying my power statements, I joyfully ring a little bell or clap my hands and communicate to my angels my wishes for a great day. I put the universe on notice that I am ready for the adventures of today. This will fill your body with energy and joy. If you start your day with positive actions and thoughts, you are one step ahead already.

Nighttime Ritual

I usually meditate for a few minutes before bedtime. I also go over the events of the day and write in my journal. I make sure that I write the good things that happened during the day, the small pleasures that I was able to enjoy, and then close my writings with gratitude for another day. If there is any forgiveness of myself or others, I go ahead and do it before my prayers.

While thanking my body for the day's work, I reward myself by massaging my body with essential oils to relax and give love and attention to myself. It is a practice that helps with sleep. If you are exhausted at night, massaging your feet and neck will be extremely beneficial. Of course, if you have a companion to assist you, it is even better and gets you in the mood for practicing receiving and giving.

Right before I fall asleep, I repeat a protection mantra and feel gratitude for all my blessings. I also generate the feeling of love and protection for the night. This is a great time to practice correct breathing to destress your body and relax completely. This special mantra is my favorite, another little present from Mother Mary on a night when I was restless and could not fall asleep. I had let a difficult situation during the day take me out of my love center.

I sleep protected by the light of the Father.
I dream content in the love of the Mother.
When morning comes, I awake in joy with the light of the Christ.

It is extremely important to have a good night's sleep. Your spiritual practice will help immensely with sleep problems. By going over the day's events, forgiving, writing, and so on, you are leaving the problems of the day behind and signaling your mind to get to the business of sleep and to get inspiration and insights during your dream time.

I have also noticed that by meditating daily, even if I get fewer hours of sleep, I feel rested and refreshed in the morning. The hours that I actually sleep are definitely quality sleep.

A Special Way to Pray

Prayer alone or in groups is a powerful instrument to access a better life. However, most people are unaware of the beauty and efficiency of this powerful tool.

Prayer is not just reciting a few words that might not even resonate with you. Prayer is a state of mind and a total knowing that you are being heard and that your petition will be handled with the most love and compassion. We have to be in the absolute knowing that our heavenly family wants the best for us.

Praying is similar to having a conversation with your very best friends and knowing that they only have your happiness in mind. If you are angry or fearful, tell your heavenly family how you feel. Share all your insecurities. It is part of our humanity to feel all those emotions, but it is part of our divinity to transform them into love and compassion for ourselves and others.

No begging or suffering is necessary to be heard, just a conversation between best friends. Feel excited and grateful that you have loving connections ready to assist you. Be convinced that the best outcome is showing up at exactly the right time.

I have discovered that one key ingredient for successful prayer is practice. Just like any other skill in life, the more you practice, the better you will become. Of course, the main ingredient is faith that you are being heard and your petitions will be handled with unconditional love and compassion.

Learning to go directly to the Creator is a long process for most people. We are all capable of reaching the Father; however, it takes wisdom and practice. Thankfully, we have many helpers along the way, as explained in the wedding feast chapter.

As above, so below. Imagine going to the White House and demanding an audience with the president. Good luck with that one. We have only copied on earth the pattern that exists in heaven. It is not that the Father sees us as not worthy of his presence; it is we who, having neglected the temple (the body), cannot access that level of clarity to reach the light.

The heavenly realm has many mansions, like Jesus said. The more we clear our communication equipment with a good spiritual practice, the sooner, of course, we can reach the ultimate mansion. In the meantime, if we are in love with 900-calorie cheeseburgers and other unhealthy habits, we better hire a good team of angels in both realities.

I direct my prayers most of the time to Mother Mary, and I am in complete trust and knowing that she is listening to me and that the answers will show up according to my divine plan and at the right time. During prayer, I also have what I call "heavenly meetings," where I ask for the assistance of all my guides. I also express my gratitude for all their help. I have come to realize that heaven has a perfect customer service and specialized departments.

I have had great results when I direct my prayers to the correct being of light.

For family matters, such as protection and guidance for children, I pray to Mother Mary. She is in charge of the entire angelic realm. If your wedding feast is running out of wine, she is definitely your right contact.

For healing of any type, I definitely go straight to the Great Physician, the Master Christ himself.

For difficult people and enemies, I pray to my adored Archangel Michael.

Some years ago, I worked with an extremely angry woman at an assisted-living facility. She was very rude to the residents, coworkers, and superiors. She had seniority and felt that she owned the facility. She made threats to anybody who did not agree with her. I felt protected by my angels, but I was worried about the residents and my coworkers who were suffering from her bullying practices. I knew that I could not confront her, so I decided to enlist Archangel Michael's help. I asked him to be with me every time I had to deal with her and to heal the situation in the best possible way.

I suggested that she needed blessings but hopefully somewhere far away from us. Within two weeks of my petition, miss angry bitch presented her resignation. A few days before delivering her resignation letter, she spoke to me and explained that she had found a position with less commuting time and more money, and she felt that this would help her decrease her stress level. She also said that I was the first person she was trusting with her news. I had to stop myself from breaking into one of my crazy dances at the outcome of this difficult situation.

Choosing me to be the first one to know was the work of Archangel Michael's sense of humor. He was delighted in seeing my predicament of keeping a straight face while she was confiding in me. I remarked that he didn't have to throw the extra money in the deal, but he reminded me that everything has a solution, and even mean people can be blessed when someone prays for them and hands the situation to heavenly hands.

The more we practice prayer, the easier it is to access that space of love where healing and answers come to us. Sometimes the answer is not what we expected, but please realize that it is always with our well-being in mind. Be thankful for every result and know that every result has a teaching wrapped around it.

One of my most memorable experiences with prayer came when I was caring for a terminally ill lady at her home. She had come home from the hospital with just a few days to live and was hoping to see relatives from out of state. These relatives were very dear to her, and they were doing their best to be with her before her passing. She was in terrible pain and did not want to be drugged at the moment of her death. Her siblings were by her side, grieving and extremely upset about her suffering and expected death.

They were devoted Catholics, and we gathered to pray and say the rosary. Someone from her church was also there to administer the sacrament of communion. It was a beautiful scene, and she was surrounded by the love of her siblings and our care and compassion. She could barely open her mouth for the communion wafer, but she was eager to accept it. Moments after communion, the entire aura of the room changed, and she looked totally transformed. She fixed her sight in a corner of the room, and she seemed aware, serene, and joyful.

We all went speechless and felt this loving energy surrounding every one of us. She was seeing something beautiful, and we were sensing it. The energy of the room that just moments before seemed sad and suffocating felt comfortable and peaceful. It even smelled different, and it was full of light and acceptance. This was a generous touch of divine love for her siblings to accept her death.

When we were back to reality, we realized that Jesus and Mother Mary had just been with us and taught us not to be afraid of death. This dear lady lasted enough hours to see her out-of-town relatives and say her goodbyes. It was a privilege being with her in her last hours on earth and being a guest to an unforgettable experience of divine love. I will always be grateful to my heavenly friends for this precious gift of honoring us with their presence and helping me understand the power of prayer and the lesson of facing death with acceptance and grace.

Of course, dying with dignity and prayer is not reserved just for Catholics. Every dying human being benefits from a gathering of loving people and compassionate prayer.

Angels at Your Service

I have always felt comfortable with angels in my life, and I considered myself blessed that heaven or earth angels always arrive to my assistance when I need them the most. My personal habit is to call for Mother Mary to send in the angels. Others feel comfortable asking Archangel Michael. They have the best customer-service training and are thrilled to get your requests.

It is of great help in life to get in the habit of employing angels always. They absolutely love to help, but we must ask first. One little secret is to be very specific with your petitions to them; they are so thrilled to help that communication can become fuzzy and sometimes even hilarious. With practice, you will know their ways.

Angels and Children

I first started employing angels on an ongoing basis when my children were little. I used to call in four angels per child to protect them during sleep. They did a wonderful job keeping my children free of nightmares and sleeping through the night.

My daughter's angels would misbehave once in a while, but I think it was because she is very intuitive, and she could see them and communicate with them. One night at around two in the morning, my three-year-old daughter walked into my room giggling and told me that they were playing and tickling her. I was puzzled but too sleepy to think straight. I assumed that she must have been dreaming and tucked her back in bed. A few nights later, she was back in my bedroom with the same story. Suddenly, my little light turned on in my sleepy brain. I remember not having been very specific with her angels when I invited them to protect my daughter.

They love children and are delighted to help them. Most children can see them up until about the age of three or four. (My youngest son tells me that he used to see a being of light standing by his bed.)

The following night, I had a long talk with them with specific instructions. I stated my petition clearly: "Make sure that you watch my daughter sleep and protect her, but *do not* awaken her to play during the night. She may be awakened at 7:00 a.m. for playtime." I thanked them for listening and for doing a great job protecting my daughter. That's all it took. From then on, she slept through the night and was wide awake and happy in the morning, ready for the day.

After my granddaughter was born, I decided that I would be available as much as possible in her life. I was working full-time but would spend my days off with her. The first time she spent the night proved to be very difficult. She was only about eighteen month old, and by bedtime, she was crying for her mother.

I immediately asked Mother Mary to send a team of angels quickly. Within a few minutes of my petition, we went to the kitchen for some water. When I handed her the cup of water, it slipped off my hands before reaching her little hands, splashing water on the kitchen floor and splashing her legs and feet.

My first thought was, *Not now. I already have enough trying to keep her happy.* But suddenly she started laughing and jumping up and down with delight. I smiled at the tactics of my angels helping me with playtime. I immediately sat her on my kitchen countertop with her little legs in the sink, and we played for hours, bathing her dolls and making bubbles. She slept through the night, and we have been having fun with water ever since.

Help While Driving

While driving, I ask the angels to come along, and I picture four angels surrounding my car. I have avoided accidents and traffic tickets by their protection. I credit my angels for my good driving record because I have no sense of direction and can get lost easily. My children used to ask, "Are we lost yet?" even before leaving our driveway. I could not even fool small children. Before I employed driving angels, my neighbors and relatives were terrified of my driving skills. There was no mailbox stand, fence, or trash container safe from my driving atrocities. I also invite my angels to travel with me when using other means of transportation or when other people are driving.

I cannot say enough about employing angels to help in our day-to-day living. One of my most memorable angel miracles came years ago. I was pregnant with my second child, and I was driving early in the evening, with my daughter asleep in her car seat. I was heading home from a children's birthday party in New Orleans, and I had to cross a lake to get to my nearby city.

I decided to take an old, narrow bridge, which was a shortcut, since I was tired and it was getting late. This was a five-mile bridge with no shoulders and poor lightning. As soon as I got on the bridge, the visibility became impossible; fog was engulfing the bridge and the lake. Traffic was light, and I could not see any lights in front of me. I was panicking and literally trembling, and with my nonexistent sense of direction, I was terrified. I took a deep breath and yelled, "Dear Mother, please send some angels fast." Instantly, I saw brilliant lights ahead of me, enough to help me see the way clearly but not blinding. My mind was trying to make sense of this and thinking that there was a really neat car ahead of me, but my soul knew that this was help from above.

I kept following this guiding light for dear life. To my complete amazement, as soon as I finished crossing the bridge and could see street and home lights, my guiding lights disappeared into thin air. There was no other vehicle around, just clear road. As soon as I got home, I prayed with a heart full of gratitude for the kindness of my heavenly family.

Help with Buying a Home

After I learned that I was going to be a grandmother, I decided to buy a little house to make it perfect for my new grandchild coming. This was a difficult task in Louisiana a few years after Hurricane Katrina, but I armed myself with the strength of my heavenly buddies. I prayed to be guided to the right house and to keep my ego in check in order to stay on my budget. I made a list of the main things that the house should have and stayed alert at reading the energy of the homes that were shown to me.

I was directed to a very patient and loving real estate professional. She understood my search. I ran from some houses just after stepping on the front entrance. I could sense that I would not be happy there. After a few months, we had found two homes in my target neighborhood, and I focused on them. I felt better energy with choice number two, but my ego wanted choice number one. House number one was elegant and updated with colorful decorating touches. House number two seemed humble, but something about that house told me that the previous owners had a happy life there.

I could see myself showing off and giving great parties in house number one, so I went ahead and made a full offer with very few demands. The real estate lady assured me that this offer could not be refused. The house had been on the market for a while, and the owner was eager to sell. To our complete surprise, the owner turned down the offer, saying he had decided to rent it out instead.

I went into an angry tirade with my heavenly buddies and went to bed upset and demanding answers from my angels. As soon as I woke up the next day, I meditated, calmed myself down, and asked for guidance. I called my Realtor immediately and told her to forget the defeat of yesterday and to go for house number two.

I made an offer with many demands and lower than the asking price. She advised me that it might take a while to get this house because the heirs were going through the usual paperwork of the inheritance. Another surprise—they accepted the offer, and the paperwork was finished quicker than everybody had imagined.

We were on final inspection one day, and I met one of my new neighbors, who told me that I would be very happy in the house. She said that the elderly couple that had lived there were the greatest people, and every repair was done with love and the best of materials. And here is the icing on the cake and my sign that it was divinely arranged: she said, "The lady was devoted to the angels." All her decorations were of angels inside and outside the house, and she showed me some of the angels that the heirs had given to her.

As I was moving in, I noticed that there was a pink, little angel figurine remaining above my kitchen door. It is beautifully carved in wood with brown hair and a chubby face. I knew that this was the confirmation that I would spend great times in this house with my beautiful granddaughter.

When she first started talking, she would point at the angel and say that it was a picture of herself, and indeed, that little pink angel resembles her, and she made the connection perfectly.

The house was child friendly, and we spent countless hours playing with the angels and having lots of fun. May the angels always watch your life, my beautiful earth angel, and every child's life on this playground called Earth. I pray that humanity wakes up soon to appreciate the precious wisdom and love that every child brings into this world.

When the time came to let go of that temporary dwelling, I asked the angels to bless the next residents and to point my way for my next adventure.

One last story of my wonderful angels came when I decided that I wanted to take a theta healing class after reading about Vianna Stibal several years ago. (She healed herself of cancer.) I came across information that she would be giving her next workshop in Heber City, Utah. The organizer explained to me that I would have to drive from the Salt Lake City airport to Heber City. I told her that I would not feel comfortable driving, but I was being led to this class for some reason, so I was going to pray about it.

I also asked her to let me know if she heard of somebody who would be landing in Salt Lake, saying that I would be more than happy to rent the car in exchange for her driving. She assured me that she would keep that in mind.

I called in my traveling angels and asked them to please make the necessary arrangements. In a couple of hours, the organizer called me back and said, "You will not believe this, but I just received a call from someone who wants to come in from San Francisco. She is on a tight budget and is very interested in sharing expenses. She says that she loves driving." What a job done by my efficient angels!

I authorized her to give the traveler my phone number, and we made the arrangements. We landed in Salt Lake City within minutes of each other. We were also blessed with a nice suite of two bedrooms in a beautiful inn, and we had the most incredible time during that weekend, learning and sharing with other people of like mind.

These are the accounts of my most memorable encounters with angels, but I experience their assistance every day of my life. I do the asking, and they willingly fulfill their mission of guidance and love. Thank you, my angels. You are the best.

GRATITUDE

My immense gratitude to Divine Mother, known to me as Mother Mary, and to my teams of angels and ascended masters.

To my loving Master Christ, thank you for your patience, unconditional love and compassion, and for the light apparitions that are your special signs and gifts to me. What a privilege to be in your company.

To the Carmelite nuns in Lacombe, Louisiana, for helping me see my way back to Mother Mary. I will never forget the centering prayer days with my beloved sister Christine and all the sisters I met in such beautiful surroundings.

Special thanks to my mother for teaching me, among other things, the discipline to read from an early age and to search for my own interpretation and truth. I know she is happy in the spirit world and communicates with me in dreams and a special sign of yellow butterflies.

My thanks to every light worker who in one way or another contributed to my journey. To all those spiritual teachers and visionaries, our time has come.

Thanks to all those women healers who graced my life, including my beautiful grandmothers and the circle of magical female healers from my childhood. I know your healing mission has never ended and your healing light is still shining from heaven.

With immense gratitude to my sister Rosa Arely for sharing the road of intuition with me. We were weird kids, but we had each other to share experiences and to be a united front against our critics. Thank you for believing in me and for encouraging me to tell my truth and reach for the sky. Our infinite love will forever shine in countless lifetimes and universes.

9 798369 421635